THE PRODUCTION OF KING OEDIPUS

An essay by

Tyrone Guthrie
and
Tanya Moiseiwitsch

Foreword by Clare Ferraby

Including interview with
Colin George *and* Tanya Moiseiwitsch

Edited by Tedd George

This essay is reproduced with the permission of the Board of Directors of the Tyrone Guthrie Centre at Annaghmakerrig and the estate of Tanya Moiseiwitsch.

All rights reserved
© 2022 Tyrone Guthrie & Tanya Moiseiwitsch

ISBN: 978-1-8384036-9-0

The rights of Sir Tyrone Guthrie and Tanya Moiseiwitsch to be identified as the authors of this work have been asserted by their estates in accordance with the Copyright, Designs & Patents Act 1988.

No part of this book may be reproduced or transmitted in any form or by any means without the written permission of Wordville.

Cover artwork: Messenger from *The Persians*,
Crucible Theatre, October 1972
by Tanya Moiseiwitsch

Proofread by Ruby Gawe

Wordville
www.wordville.net
info@wordville.net

TYRONE GUTHRIE

Sir Tyrone Guthrie (1900–71) was a towering figure of international theatre who was highly influential in his lifetime. Describing himself as 'a very Irish sort of Anglo-Scot', Guthrie built his reputation in the 1930s as a versatile director, scoring critical and commercial successes with his productions of Shakespeare, opera and plays by new or unknown playwrights.

Guthrie was a pioneer of the thrust stage, a re-imagining of Ancient Greek and Shakespearean theatre, with the actors playing on an open stage with the audience surrounding them on three sides.

After successfully experimenting with the thrust stage at the second Edinburgh Festival in 1948, Guthrie collaborated with designer Tanya Moiseiwitsch to create a thrust stage for the inaugural festival in Stratford, Ontario in 1953. He co-wrote this essay with her about their production of *Oedipus* in the second season.

Encouraged by this success, in 1963 Guthrie founded the Guthrie Theater in Minneapolis, which also had a thrust stage designed by Tanya. He served as the theatre's Artistic Director until 1966. Guthrie was also the inspiration for other thrust stage theatres, including the Festival Theatre Chichester, the Octagon Theatre (Perth, Australia) and the Crucible Theatre (Sheffield, UK).

Guthrie died in April 1971, only a few months before the Crucible opened.

Tyrone Guthrie (1956)

Tanya Moiseiwitsch (1948)

TANYA MOISEIWITSCH

Tanya Moiseiwitsch (1914-2003) was a pioneering figure of theatre design whose career spanned more than half a century. Born in London, she was the daughter of Benno Moiseiwitsch, a renowned classical pianist and the Australian concert violinist, Daisy Kennedy.

After studying at the Central School of Art and Design, Tanya joined the Old Vic as a scene-painter during Tyrone Guthrie's first season in 1933. She went on to become the designer of numerous productions for Guthrie at the Old Vic, the Memorial Theatre in Stratford-upon-Avon and on Broadway. Tanya was also a designer at the Abbey Theatre, Dublin (1935-39), where she designed more than 50 productions.

In 1953 Guthrie invited Tanya to design a new theatre for the inaugural festival in Stratford, Ontario, which would have a thrust stage. Working with Guthrie, Tanya developed her trademark design for the thrust stage, which she further refined at the Guthrie Theater (1963) and the Crucible Theatre (1971).

Aside from her work with Guthrie, Tanya designed productions at the National Theatre, the Royal Opera House, the Metropolitan Opera (New York) and on Broadway. At one point in her career, five productions she had designed were running in London at the same time.

Tanya Moiseiwitsch died in May 2003.

TABLE OF CONTENTS

Foreword by Clare Ferraby   v

Editor's Note by Tedd George   viii

List of illustrations   x

The Production of *King Oedipus*: An essay
by Tyrone Guthrie and Tanya Moiseiwitsch   1

Cast of *King Oedipus*, 1954   83

Interview with Tanya Moiseiwitsch
and Colin George, May 2001   85

FOREWORD by Clare Ferraby

I first met Tanya Moiseiwitsch in 1968 when she was working on the design of the Crucible Theatre in Sheffield. By then, Tanya was renowned as a pioneering figure in theatre design, both for her highly original costume design and also for her collaboration with Tyrone Guthrie on the thrust stage theatres at Stratford, Ontario and in Minneapolis. Like few others at the time or since, Tanya had a clear understanding of how the thrust stage worked. There was only nominal use of scenery, relying on the disposition of actors in three dimensional formats, their rapid entrances and exits through her specially designed tunnels ('vomitoria') under the audience, with costumes of stunning concept and originality including stilts and masks, thus achieving scale and hierarchy.

The fortunate arrival of Guthrie in Sheffield when discussions over the nature of the new theatre were at a critical juncture led to my introduction to this legendary female figure. My husband, architect Nick Thompson, was appointed to lead the team charged with creating a new generation of thrust stage theatre in Sheffield. Although he had no previous experience of theatre design, he had the great fortune to work closely with Tanya who was appointed as design consultant and who helped guide him and the client through the design process, which stemmed from the shape of the stage itself.

My training at Sheffield and Manchester, along with my experience working in various European design studios, encouraged Nick to involve me in the development of the colour scheme for the interior of the new theatre complex. Only a few standard dire colours were available at that time, which meant creating new colours, and I designed a highly innovative abstract striped carpet, created from two carpets sewn together; both of these designs set manufacturers new challenges to meet my concept.

It was therefore with some trepidation as a young designer that I first met the illuminating figure of Tanya Moiseiwitsch, who fortunately endorsed my vision. I was immediately impressed by Tanya's gentleness, her empathy and understanding with her colleagues, and her decisiveness and positivity in achieving design aims. For me it was rare to find a fellow female artist who had such confidence in innovation and its outcome.

Her incredible attention to detail of size, depth, material, texture and tonal values were aspects of true design that were close to my own approach. There was a clarity of overall vision, and an approach that supported colleagues in their jobs and, if they didn't achieve what was needed, then get on with it yourself. Typically, Tanya would not give me the critical specification for the finish to the stage floor of the new thrust stage auditorium in Sheffield, despite being asked several times. I eventually saw her on her hands and knees on the new stage, meticulously achieving her desired effect by painting it herself.

For me, Tanya was an inspirational colleague whose friendship and generosity was to last for the rest of her life. We would jointly celebrate our birthdays (which are on adjoining days). One year she gave me a much-prized present: a long magnificently embroidered silk Chinese tea gown that had belonged to her Drinkwater relative. Tanya inspired an entire generation of female theatre designers, among them Elaine Garrard and Alison Chitty, and she gave me the resolve to develop my own career in the broadest aspect of theatre design.

Reading this essay written by Tanya and Guthrie many years after it was written, I was struck by how it captures their joint approach to designing for the thrust stage: innovative, practical and considering the needs of both the audience and the actors. It was to lay the groundwork for what was to become her masterpiece, the Crucible Theatre in Sheffield, and influenced much of Nick's and my subsequent theatre design work together.

Clare Ferraby
London, 2022

EDITOR'S NOTE by Tedd George

The essay reproduced in this book was written by Tyrone Guthrie and Tanya Moiseiwitsch for the third in a series of books about the Festival Theatre Stratford, Ontario. It was commissioned following the critical success of their production of *Oedipus* in 1954, which resulted in a world tour of the production and a film in 1957, as well as laying the groundwork for their subsequent work on Ancient Greek drama, notably their interpretation of the *Oresteia*, called *The House of Atreus* (at the Guthrie Theater & on national tour, 1966-68).

I first came across this essay while editing the manuscript by my late father, Colin George, about the battle to build the Crucible Theatre. Guthrie sent my father a copy of the original typescript as inspiration for his own production of *Oedipus* at the Sheffield Playhouse in 1968, and its influence was evident, with an all-male cast playing in Greek masks and the heroes wearing platform boots. I immediately recognised it as one of the great lost essays on theatre. Rarely have I read an account of the preparations for a theatre production that so fully captures the creative process and the challenges faced by the director, the designers and the actors. These range from the symbolic (how should we interpret Oedipus blinding himself?) to the practical (how does an actor perform when their face is covered by a mask with a fixed expression?)

I was determined to make this essay available to modern readers, and I am grateful to the Tyrone Guthrie Centre at

Annaghmakerrig and to the estate of Tanya Moiseiwitsch for giving their permission to republish it in this book. My thanks also go to Clare Ferraby for writing the foreword, and to my publisher (and sister) Lucy for steering this passion project to print.

To give some context to the essay, I have included the transcript of my father's interview with Tanya in May 2001, where they discuss the origins of Stratford, Ontario's thrust stage and their work together, along with a selection of Tanya's designs from the original production of *Oedipus* and of her work with Guthrie and my father.

I hope that this essay will offer readers fresh insights into *Oedipus* and serve as inspiration for new theatrical interpretations of Sophocles' greatest work.

Tedd George
London, 2022

All the images in this book come from the George Family Archive. They are reproduced with the permission of the estate of Tanya Moiseiwitsch and the Crucible Theatre, Sheffield.

LIST OF ILLUSTRATIONS

1. Conceptual design for King Oedipus with crown and sceptre, by Tanya Moiseiwitsch
2. Conceptual design for Queen Jocasta, by Tanya Moiseiwitsch
3. Conceptual design for mask of Creon, by Tanya Moiseiwitsch
4. Design of Tiresias, by Tanya Moiseiwitsch
5. Conceptual design of the Priest, by Tanya Moiseiwitsch
6. James Mason as Oedipus, Stratford, Ontario, 1954
7. Donald Davis as Tiresias, Stratford, Ontario, 1954
8. Tony Van Bridge as the Man from Corinth, costume and masks designed by Tanya Moiseiwitsch and Jacqueline Cundall
9. William Needles as the Old Shepherd, Stratford, Ontario, 1954
10. *The Thrie Estaits* at the Assembly Hall, Edinburgh, 1948
11. Two views of the auditorium of the Festival Theatre, Stratford, Ontario, which replaced 'The Tent' in 1957 and which was modified in 1962
12. Poster for *Oedipus the King* and *Oedipus at Colonus*, Adelaide State Theatre Company, 1978
13. Tanya Moiseiwitsch's central design for *The Persians* at the Crucible Theatre (Sheffield), October 1972
14. Tanya Moiseiwitsch's designs for the Messenger over the years: *King Oedipus* (1954), *The House of Atreus* (1967), *The Persians* (1972) and *Oedipus The King* (1978)

THE PRODUCTION OF KING OEDIPUS

by

TYRONE GUTHRIE

and

TANYA MOISEIWITSCH

PREPARATION FOR A PRODUCTION

THE PROCESS of preparation which precedes the production of a play varies very considerably with the nature of the play, and with the conditions—time, place, budget and so on—which govern the production. In this essay, then, rather than attempt any generalised description, we have concentrated on the preparation of one particular production which had interested us very much: the *Oedipus* of Sophocles. Much has already been written about this play. Historians, literary and dramatic critics, moralists, psychologists and poets have for centuries discussed it from their different points of view; they will continue to do so for centuries more. As is so often the case where dramatic literature is concerned, little or nothing has been written about methods of realising the work in performance.

Without wishing in any way to belittle the contributions of learned men, one regrets that from the vast mass of scholarly criticism of dramatic literature it is not possible to get a clearer idea of what performances of *Oedipus* have been like. Who would not gladly trade many millions of words of grammarians' wrangling for a detailed, technical account of, say, the original production of even such comparatively recent works as *The Beggar's Opera* or *She Stoops to Conquer?* How much it would tell us not only about theatrical practice and outlook at the time, about changing public taste, but about the works themselves. And how much more valuable still would such information be about works of more remote date where even less is known about the public and theatrical context of their production. Quite apart from the technical interest of such accounts, they would illuminate a point which often eludes grammarians, that is the extraordinary influence of fashion upon the interpretation of a classic. In the light of contemporary attitudes to social and moral issues, a play can have a number of entirely different *meanings*; and works which seem lively and interesting in one period are bores in another.

The practitioner's approach is sometimes, but not always, unintelligent, often slapdash, often over-influenced by design to please audiences, which are more susceptible to shock tactics than to finesse. And, though the practitioner is not immune from exhibitionism, yet neither is the scholar. Also, we cannot help feeling that the practitioner's point of view is apt to be more lively than the scholar's because his theories must be submitted to the test of practice. They may not on that account be valid, but they are likely to avoid the worst excesses of pedantic niggling and learned silliness.

The following discussion of *Oedipus* must not, therefore, be regarded as anything other than the groping and fumbling approach of two collaborators who make no claim to scholarship, but only to some considerable practical experience in the theatre, and to a right to interpret this masterpiece according to their own limited but enthusiastic lights.

THE FACTS OF THE PLAY

TO UNDERSTAND ANY PLAY it is necessary to make clear to the audience the facts which it relates. Drama is storytelling first and last, storytelling in its most direct form. The characters of drama are impersonated by people who recapitulate the story in words and in action.

With any story of serious intentions, however, the mere facts—what happens next—are not important. The point is the style or manner in which it is told, and the comment which it attempts to make upon life and mankind in general. The story of the Prodigal Son, for instance, is not important so much because of what happens, but because very briefly, very memorably, very poignantly, it makes a number of shrewd comments upon the relation of all fathers to all sons, including that of a Heavenly Father to Prodigal Humanity.

An author need not necessarily be aware of the comment he is making. In fact, the most important and interesting comments frequently emerge without the author's conscious awareness, sometimes even in spite of his conscious intention to the contrary. Moreover, the same work may be very differently interpreted by different people and at different times, and such difference does not necessarily imply that one comment is more valid than another. Broadly speaking, the greatest works of art are susceptible to the greatest variety of interpretation; they do not fully reveal themselves to any one person at any one time.

Sophocles wrote *King Oedipus* about 254 B.C. It was entered for the great dramatic contest which was the centrepiece of the Spring Festival in which Athens honoured the god, Dionysus. Note that Dionysus is not, however, an important deity in the play which is dominated by Apollo. This may be because neither Sophocles nor most of his very sophisticated audience any longer believed literally in the existence of a heavenly family in which all the gods were 'children' or Zeus and Hera who dwelt literally on Mount Olympus and whose family life was a tumult of human passion uninhibited by the physical limitations of human beings. It is not unreasonable to suppose that Sophocles may have felt about the Olympians very much as a thoughtful man of our own day feels about the ferocious deity who dominates the Book of Judges: a conception of godhead which we believe to be a primitive one, which subsequent and more sophisticated societies have softened and rendered more subtle, have made to conform more closely to their own ideals. For it can hardly be denied that though we profess to believe that God created us in his image, none the less we create Him for ourselves in ours.

The aspect of Deity with which Sophocles is concerned in this play is Apollo, the God of Light, and thence, metaphorically, the God of Knowledge, of Revelation, of Intuition and Inspiration; the Sun God and therefore the source not merely of light but also of heat, or fertility—in short, a conception very little removed from any reasonable person's embodiment of Omnipotence and Immanence, a conception which is no less, and no more, acceptable now than it must have been 2,000 years ago.

Now it is necessary to recall briefly how the Athenian Festival of Dionysus came into being. In all epochs and in all climates the return of spring after winter has been, for obvious reasons, an occasion of thankfulness and joy. In very primitive society, man expressed his emotion spontaneously and instinctively. Gradually his spontaneous reaction to the unexpected return of warmth and fertility was replaced by an annually recurrent, remembered and looked-forward-to joy, tempered by thankfulness to the Origin of the miracle. This recurrent and more sophisticated reaction resulted in recurrent and more sophisticated expressions and emotion. Moreover, the recurrent season of fertility induced primitive man not only to feel but to act. There were seeds to sow in the earth. Man, the sun's image, feeling the joy and vigour of spring in his body, nourished again after a winter of short commons, must plant his own seed in the body of Woman, the image of the Earth. Rain must be prayed for, begged, induced to fall and fertilize the earth. It is not hard to guess the very broad outlines of primitive rites of spring. These rites in Athens were focussed on Dionysus, an impersonation of joyous intoxication, of many ideas and emotions associated with fertility, liberation from bondage, the relations of male with female.

For the purpose of this essay, we need not discuss in detail the Dionysiac rites, except to say that generations before Sophocles they included the sacrifice of a beast, itself almost certainly a symbolic substitute for the human sacrifice of still earlier times. The story of Abraham and Isaac is an interesting parable of precisely such a process. In the story as related in Genesis the beast is miraculously substituted for the human. As so often, a miracle accounts *tout à coup* for an individual change of heart which normally occurs collectively over a span of many generations, a slow process of social and moral evolution.

Gradually, as Athens became richer and softer and gentler, public opinion was repelled by the public slaughter even of a lamb or a kid; and, by a still further process of substitution, the sacrifice was now merely enacted ritually by priests in narrative and mime. One cannot but be reminded of the Christian rite of Holy Communion, where the human sacrifice of Christ—the breaking of the body and the spilling of the blood of the Lamb of God—is re-enacted by a priest in narrative and by the symbolical breaking of bread and pouring of wine. Even in the time of Sophocles, sacrifice was already expressed by narrative and mime which was no longer literally concerned with ritual slaughter. Tragedy was considered to pay sufficient tribute to the god by recapitulating half-secular legends on the *theme* of suffering.

Just as the participants at Holy Communion commemorate Christ's sacrifice, so, presumably, the Athenian audience at the Dionysiac Festival partook of the Passion there commemorated. Reverent spectators of the Passion of Oedipus will surely have felt their own 'communion' with his agony.

THE CHOICE OF TRANSLATION

AT AN EARLY STAGE of preparation it was necessary to decide which translation of the play should be used. The choice was bewildering, but fairly soon two main alternatives emerged. Some translators were primarily concerned with being faithful to the original text of Sophocles, and only secondarily interested in the effect of their own version. Others were prepared to sacrifice exact correspondence with the author's literal meaning in order to make his general intention more acceptable.

We plumped for the second school of thought. The literal translations were, most of them, barely readable; and when spoken aloud the effect was positively absurd—clumsy, unrhythmic, unmelodious sentences that bore no relation to human utterance.

So many scholars have supposed that the meaning of a play can be abstracted from its form that, in this play for instance, the speeches can be rendered in a form which is not only utterly unmusical but, in its laudable desire to be faithful, almost unintelligible. This arises because many scholars never think, even reject with repugnance, the idea that a play has been written to be acted, that its lines are the score of a symphony. To many scholars great plays are 'texts' first and last, to be absorbed by the intelligence alone and unassisted by the senses, except for the use of eyes to interpret the letters of the printed page. Again and again, instances arise of Shakespearean scholars who because of their blindness and deafness to theatrical effect, and because of their childlike ignorance of how and why theatrical effects are produced, miss implications, labour the obvious and, in short, make asses of themselves. Scholars, with no less justification, level exactly analogous charges at those who think theatrical skills and experience suffice without scholarship. The one point of view is as foolishly narrow as the other.

Of the English translations which have some pretension as dramatic literature, by far the best known are those of Gilbert Murray.[1] His version of *Oedipus* is melodious, swings along on rhythms that are easy on the ear; his introduction to his version gives a considerable clue to the translator's intentions and personality and is a little masterpiece of its kind, a rare combination of modesty with learning, of learning with philosophy and philosophy with common sense. It may well be that Murray's translations will become the classic English versions of Euripides and even of Sophocles. But for us now his flowing and 'beautiful' translation conjures up only euphoric and scented Mediterranean visions of Leighton or Albert Moore.[2] In this landscape one could only see plump, pretty, pink Englishwomen in 'Greek' fancy-dress in mauves and pinks and palest yellow, and under-graduates who, momentarily laying aside their cricket bats, were making believe, in very upper-class accents, to be Old Men of Thebes. The Murray version, in short seemed to us to

---

[1] Gilbert Murray (1866-1957) was a classical scholar and leading authority on the culture of Ancient Greece.
[2] Frederic Leighton (1830-1896) and Albert Moore (1841-1893) were English painters known for their depictions of languorous female figures in idyllic Mediterranean settings.

have sacrificed, in favour of a rather [eighteen] ninety-ish 'beauty', too much of the impersonal and removed grandeur of the original. While this may well be unimportant, it seemed to us dated. This may mean no more than that its particular kind of poetry and particular kind of drama are very temporarily out of fashion, and will come in again quite soon. It is not necessarily a condemnation of a work of art because from time to time it goes out of vogue. But if in the theatre one prepares a production of a work which *feels* out of date, there is every danger that the production will be dowdy and dreary. Respect and reverence alone do not generate the energy which is required to put a difficult play upon the stage. There must be enthusiasm. If enthusiasm is not there, then the task is better not attempted.

Of translations into English more modern than Murray's, the best seemed to us that of Watling,[3] published in the late thirties, and an earlier one made for production in Dublin by the great Irish poet, William Butler Yeats. Of these two Watling's had the advantage of being far closer to Sophocles, far closer both literally and in intention. Yeats has made no attempt to 'translate'; he has retained the main structure of the original but has omitted whole passages whose meaning seemed to him to have become obscured by distance. He has made no attempt to

---

[3] E. F. Watling was an English schoolmaster, classicist and translator. He produced translations for Penguin Classics of Sophocles' three Theban plays, nine plays of Plautus and a selection of Seneca's tragedies.

reproduce the literary or dramatic style of Sophocles. He has missed much that Watling and other translators have attempted and often achieved. But of all the very many translations which we read, only that of Yeats succeeded in rendering the choruses so that the English versions were poems in their own right.

The Yeats choruses, though often quite far removed from the original, have a logic which reinforces the music and a music which reinforces the logic; the poems provide the necessary logical and musical bridge from one dramatic episode to another. We could imagine that in Yeats' version the Chorus could make a contribution to the performance which would be dynamic and not either just sentimental or else a difficult and interruptious bore.

Except for the choruses, the Yeats version is in prose; prose of a stern simplicity; prose of military terseness and practicality. The poet has been at pains to exclude anything that might seem to be added ornament or colour or artifice. There are hardly any similes, a minimum of descriptive adjectives; no high-falutin' poetical words are used; all the familiar clichés and dodges of rhetoric are eschewed. This makes of it a very aristocratic, but austere and uncompromising document; it treads barefoot over steep sharp rocks. Compared to it, Murray's is a rum-ti-tumpty of purpurate passage through meadows of asphodel azured with amaranth, down to a sea that is silver in starlight.

Yeats had made the instrument that seemed to us to fit the job. This gaunt prose suited the huge, abstracted, slightly grotesque figures which we were beginning to imagine; by being unadorned it was the more intelligible;

because the expression was brief and simple, it was not less but more moving. Above all, in this version it was possible to imagine the events of the play almost completely divorced from detail of time and place.

THE UNIVERSAL QUALITY

THIS ABSTRACT QUALITY was exactly what we wanted. We were anxious to suggest that King Oedipus was not merely the King of Thebes, the head and father of his people, but was the image of the sacrificed beast, and thence an image of human sacrifice: the one man whose death was expedient for the people. It seemed to us highly significant that the 'death' of Oedipus was not literal extinction but that he was reserved for a mysterious and incredible end, like Enoch, or for that matter like Jesus Christ, whose Passion was succeeded by a mysterious Resurrection, and that in turn by a no less mysterious Ascension. Moreover, it seemed to us highly significant that the Passion of Oedipus was expressed by self-blinding, by cutting himself off from the light. In this play the close analogy between light and God is inescapable. By destroying his own faculty of sight, by putting out the light of the eye, he was destroying the light within himself. And since, metaphorically, he was abhorring and rejecting his own insight, the recognition of his own identity, he was, both literally and metaphorically, destroying, or trying to destroy, a part of the god Apollo immanent in himself.

Again, the analogy with Christian theology struck us. The victim had God within himself; this was not merely the Passion of a man, and an emblem of mankind, but also the Passion of a god. It seemed to be the expiation by God of a crime committed by his creature man, in whom was godhead immanent. What crime? What original sin?

We shall go back to this question at the end of this essay. Meantime let us pause and consider some of the results of our conclusions so far, in the practical terms of theatrical production.

This was not to be a story about a king called Oedipus, who ruled over a city called Thebes in an identifiable locality at some vague but still identifiable date. Oedipus was to represent a far more general conception, something that was concerned with manhood in general, King Humanity.

There must, therefore, be no *literal* suggestion, in the picture which we would set before the audience, of locality or date. Since the names of people and places were Greek, and since the script is full of suggestions that the tale is to be regarded as one of great antiquity, going back into the very roots of time and the springtime of the world, we decided that the clothes should suggest, but not literally copy, the heavy folds and severe lines of early Greek sculpture. For a time, we considered the notion of a colour scheme in tender juicy greens and yellows which would literally suggest the springtime of the world, the Return of Dionysus, which would be in ironical contrast to the plague-stricken city, the doomed and ominous atmosphere which hangs over the whole play.

On second or maybe third, fourth or fifth thoughts, this idea was rejected. It would result in a trivial look, we thought, too pretty and sophisticated; the play would look vogueish; the irony would misfire. We would plump for a sombre scheme but not, we hoped, one which would lose all suggestion of radiance. This was after all a play not only about darkness, but equally about light. Oedipus, Jocasta and Creon must be royal. The Chorus must be ordinary, humble in the face of royalty. Their humility must itself exalt the mightiness of the great ones; their behaviour must suggest the critical servility of man to God; the critical servility of dogs to men.

Tiresias? The Messenger? They must wait. The main scheme must be determined. The main framework once decided, they could be fitted in.

THE CENTRAL FIGURE

OUR MINDS RETURNED TO THE CENTRAL FIGURE. Oedipus must suggest a king, a man, all men and yet no single man. He must also suggest his affinity with God—the particular aspect of godhead with which this play concerns itself—the God of light, the Sun. The Sun! He must be gold; wear a gold dress, a great gold crown with spiky rays, a sceptre of gold, a golden face.

Suddenly we apprehended that the only way we could get the feeling of universality, as opposed to particularity, of all men and yet no man was by hiding the faces of the actors, supressing their own individual traits, obliterating their small particularities behind the impersonal, but not inexpressive, features of a mask. Suddenly we realised that this was one reason, if not the dominant one, why the

Greek actors were masked—to obliterate particularity. Negatively, the actors must *not* suggest particularity; no detail of personality must intervene between the audience and the tragic symbol. Positively, they must preserve the anonymity, the aloofness, of a priest celebrating mass. So far as possible they must be mere channels through whom the effluence of something greater than ordinary human stature might pass. And then we asked ourselves whether the use of the cothurnus[4] to make them of greater than human stature was not equally indispensable. The great ones must be literally greater than their fellows.

We resolved, then, to experiment with high shoes, and with masks. About the former we had few serious doubts. There could be no insuperable practical difficulty, since the action of the tragedy never demanded any rapid movement. The masks were a more debatable problem. Could actors speak audibly from behind a mask? Would the immobility of the mask, after its first impact, become a bore?

Doubt was reinforced by the fact that the role of Oedipus was being played by James Mason. It seemed perverse to engage one of the handsomest actors of the day and then hide him behind a mask. It also seemed unreasonable to proceed any further without letting him know what we were planning. To succeed, the experiment would require the enthusiastic co-operation not only of

---

[4] A cothurnus (or buskin) is a high thick-soled laced boot worn by actors in Greek and Roman tragic drama.

Conceptual design for King Oedipus
with crown and sceptre, by Tanya Moiseiwitsch

Conceptual design for Queen Jocasta, by Tanya Moiseiwitsch

those who were to make the masks, but also of those who were to wear them.

We wrote to Mason, told him the reasons for wanting masks, expressed our doubts, made it clear that we should not push him into a mask against his will but that we rather hoped he would be interested in the experiment. He replied at once, with characteristic modesty, that he would feel more confidence, not less, if he could attempt this extremely exacting role in the heaviest possible disguise.

We decided to go ahead. We agreed that it would be practical, by thickening the soles of their shoes, to raise the actors four to six inches higher than their natural height. The masks should be even larger in relation to the size of the natural face. We resolved to experiment with masks one-and-a-half times life size. This would, we realised, make Oedipus, Creon and Jocasta appear to be creatures with disproportionately large heads. The distortion was deliberate. The large heads, we believed, would create the desired effect of rather strange greatness and impressiveness, would be another means of achieving the same aim as the judge's wig, the bishop's mitre, the guardsman's bearskin, the monarch's crown. In almost all ceremonial costume there is an attempt to enlarge and dignify the wearer by means of a sizable and heavily emphasized headpiece. Paradoxically, it is also the case that dignity is enhanced, not lost, when the headpiece verges on the grotesque, the inappropriate, the absurd. What, for example, could be more wildly unsuitable as a hat for a young girl than the British Imperial Crown? Yet it was precisely this unsuitability which enormously added to the poignancy, the dignity, the significance of the central moment of the coronation ceremony of Queen Elizabeth the Second.

Since Oedipus was to come as a golden sun, it seemed to us logical that Jocasta should be a silver figure related to the moon. Creon, just less than of royal stature, later to turn tyrant, should be of baser metal—a head and robes of dark bronze.

Now, after two productions, we feel that, whatever the result may be been, the *plan* for Oedipus and Creon was a sound one. About Jocasta we have had second thoughts. She should not have been a silver figure related to the moon, quite apart from how this particular silver mask was designed and made. That idea is too cold, too chaste and too metallic. She should have been an earth-figure—warm in colouring, soft in contour; Mother Earth, the bride of the fertilising Sun.

As it was, our original conception was that the great personages should look metallic in contrast to the Chorus who should wear life-size masks of a texture which should suggest wood or carved nuts, in dresses whose subdued low tones and soft folds should suggest, though not in a literal way, wooden figures corroded by moss and lichen, battered and twisted by winds and rain and frost.

So much for the general idea of the visual impression. The same consideration about the play would also govern its musical interpretation: absence of particularity, a removed grandeur. Obviously, something was called for [that was] larger and simpler than the life-size speech of ordinary conversation. The almost chanted declamation of

French tragedy seemed in some ways appropriate. But it did not agree too happily with the austere simplicity of Yeats, and, with its boldly sustained vowels and powerfully accented consonants, it seemed too overwhelming for the intimate conditions of our theatre. Declamation which is impressive when spouted over footlights across an orchestra pit into a great Opera House would, even if brilliantly achieved, only be embarrassing in an auditorium where the remotest spectator sits only sixteen rows back and where the nearest sit, literally, at the actors' feet. And could it be brilliantly achieved? A style so sophisticatedly classical did not seem to exploit the virtues nor conceal the shortcomings of our company.

It was decided that we would try to evolve our own style in rehearsal. Obviously, it must be more operatic and less natural than would be appropriate for Shakespeare; less so than the French style. We had at command some splendid voices, a highly intelligent, serious and flexible group of actors, a corporate spirit out of which something interesting might evolve.

It is not for us to say whether the eventual style of speech was successful or no. But we think it was reasonably consistent to a single convention, and that the Chorus had extraordinary discipline without all individuality being ironed out of the performers, and extraordinary vigour without being coarse. This was achieved only by many hours of rehearsal in the most favourable conditions, most of the time on the stage, much of the time in costume, in an atmosphere freed from a great deal of the strain and anxiety and haste attendant upon production for the commercial theatre; the kind of conditions which are all too rarely encountered, and which are only made possible by such an organisation as the Stratford Festival.

THE MAKING OF THE MASKS

IN ORDER THAT THE SPEAKING should not be impeded, the masks would cover only the upper part of their wearers' faces. Beards on the actors' chins and jaws would meet matching beards and hair on the masks. The modelling of the faces was kept extremely simple. These were not to be realistic but heavily stylized faces. Realistic masks, we considered, would not avoid the particularity of real faces. What we envisaged were masks which were no more than symbols of faces.

At one time we had the notion of making Picasso-like faces—two eyes on one side of a great triangular nose and that sort of thing. This we discarded as being obtrusive, claiming attention and interpretation on its own account.

We settled for faces whose contours and expressions were very simple and easily apprehensible. The mask for Oedipus, for instance, was intended to be the simplest possible statement of intelligence and nobility in a context of suffering.

The Chorus masks, being life-size, enabled the actors to look through the eyes of the mask. In the great masks the eye holes were far above the actor's own eyes. Gauzed apertures in the cheeks of the masks made peepholes for their wearers.

Since we considered it impossible to put 'real' hair on faces which looked like metal or wood, the wigs and beards were made of tow, string or felt, curled and twisted to look gnarled, severe or majestic as the expression of the mask demanded. Before the sketches were made, Jacqueline Cundall, the head of the Property Department at Stratford, was called in at the earliest stage of planning, and various materials were discussed. We had primarily to consider the comfort of the actors who would be wearing the masks in a tent at the height of summer under tremendous hot lamps. The masks must not only be light in weight but durable, to withstand sweat pouring down the actors' faces. It was finally decided to make them of chamois leather. Jacqueline Cundall had considerable experience in mask-making, and studied every angle of the sketches, keeping closely in touch with us over the important questions of proportion and expression. The designs for the masks grew from rough sketches which had been made in Rome of terracotta figures in the Villa Giulia, early Etruscan in date. These sketches were developed into working drawings of un-naturalistic but individual expressions of the characters as the ideas for the production became clear. Specifically, Creon has, on his first entrance, to signify that he is the bearer of good news by wearing a crown of laurel. This motif was used to represent not only a crown but the hair and beard of the figure, and the laurel was not naturalistically represented but seemed, like the head, to be moulded in bronze.

Conceptual design for mask of Creon, by Tanya Moiseiwitsch

The Old Shepherd bears some resemblance to the traditional Greek mask of a satyr, but with curly fringes of wool; we wanted to suggest that he had become like one of his own sheep.

Huge quantities of clay and plaster of Paris were delivered to the Property Department and gradually the room became crowded with clay heads swathed in damp cloths. Almost daily we were asked to compare the sketches with the newly-modelled heads before the clay hardened. Once the plaster casts were taken and the leather pressed firmly into the greased moulds, it would have been unreasonable to ask for an alteration in style or size. This, however, happened in one case. The Man from Corinth, when he came out of the mould, surprised us with a cruel, mean expression, and had to be rebuilt on kinder, more benign lines.

It could be seen at an early stage that the thirty-three masks could not possibly be ready for rehearsal, and this presented another problem. The process of modelling and making masks is of necessity a slow one, although somewhat speeded up by a specially contrived drying tent fitted with powerful lamps. It was essential for the actors to become accustomed not only to wearing masks but to seeing on each other the expressions they could achieve by tilting, bowing or raising their heads. The Property Department decided to divert some of its time and attention to making papier-mâché replicas of the masks, with a cartoon suggestion of hair painted in sepia, no time being wasted on colouring or on 'mocking-up' wigs and beards.

As the play took shape day by day these pale grey faces became familiar to us all while the work progressed in the Property Shop. Actors were called for frequent, long and troublesome fittings which were conducted in a most amiable manner; and, considering the hot summer weather, this showed remarkable tact and co-operation on the part of all concerned. Jacqueline Cundall prepared the way with the utmost confidence.

It is perhaps not easy to realise how much tact is required mutually of actors, designers and technicians at fittings. The actor is inevitably over-conscious of what he considers his own physical shortcomings. Moreover, there is always a discrepancy between the image of his 'character' which has formed in his imagination and the image which confronts him in the fitting-room looking glass. Sometimes the surprise is a pleasant one; but it is still a surprise. It is not mere vanity which makes an actor fussy at fittings. The clothes are an essential part of the character he will present. They must not only look right, they must feel right. Likewise, the designer is apt to be anxious that the designed garments should suit and please the wearer, and that the design should show to advantage on the stage. This can only be so if it is worn with appropriate style. Both parties, then, have to be careful not to allow ruffled feelings to be transferred to the tailor, and not to blame the maker for what may be faults of the design or the actor's inability to wear the dress with an air.

Opera singers, trained to use their ears but not their eyes, are the designer's bane. Hats designed for the back of the head will be pressed down onto the bridge of the nose;

it is nothing for an opera singer to put on a dress back to front, to omit essential parts of a costume, or to add little personal touches, a bow here or a frill there, an Aberdeen terrier in brilliants pinned to the front of a medieval wimple. We both know an opera chorister who used habitually to appear at matinées of *Madam Butterfly* wearing a thick tweed coat and skirt under her kimono. She did this in order to have time to get home between matinée and evening performances to give her aged mother her tea. Not unreasonably, this seemed to her important, and the fact that she looked to the audience like the wrath of God worried her not at all. But also not unreasonably, it worried the designer very much.

At fittings, tact on the part of the designer often has to verge on hypocrisy. A dumpy person with a short thick neck cannot always be truthfully told why his collar is designed in a certain style, or why the lines of the dress tend to be vertical not horizontal. If he has any sense, he will realise. But too few of us have any sense, and too many of us have no dispassionate idea whatever of our own appearance. The handsomest and best built are often the most acutely conscious of inferiority; the gawkiest and plainest specimens are frequently, and mercifully, convinced that they are Venus or Adonis.

Always it must be remembered that the design is nothing without the co-operation of its makers. The morale of the wardrobe staff is no less important than that of the company. It is the director's duty to make every actor, from the leading man down to the humblest understudy, feel that he is making a contribution that is not only indispensable but valued; similarly the designer must see that every member of the wardrobe staff, from the chief cutter down to the little middle-aged lady who sits at a machine and runs up the very plainest seams for petticoats, is credited for good work and allowed to feel an indispensable part of an essentially co-operative effort.

But again the design for a dress is nothing without the co-operation of its wearer. If the wearer is not given confidence, does not feel happy and easy in the dress, then the dress is a failure. An excellent design can be ruined if its wearer has caught in the mirror a glance of despair, even a flicker of anxiety pass between the designer and the cutter. That is why the atmosphere of fittings is important. There need be no gross flattery, but it is vital that there be an air of mutual consideration and respect, and a mutual confidence that all will be well. That is why, in the particular context of these masks, we feel grateful to Miss Cundall for her air of unwavering self-confidence and calm, and to the actors for being gay and co-operative in the early stages of fittings when the masks looked ridiculous and felt uncomfortable. The whole experience absolutely depended upon their agreeing to co-operate in a plan which seemed likely at best to eclipse their personalities, and at worst to make them look absolute fools.

At Stratford the actors made light of the inevitable discomfort of covering their faces, and appreciated the plans made for their clear seeing, hearing and speaking. Inside the leather mask there was a Perspex headband, which, resting on the actor's brows, tilted the mask so that it fitted as nearly as possible against the contours of the human face. After the beards and stylised wigs had been made and fitted, the masks were painted with subtle shading to stress the planers and angles, in the colours and tones representing wood or metal as planned in the sketches.

At the final fitting, when the draped hood matching the costume was fixed to the top of the mask, there was a feeling of wonder that the actor's personality was not submerged but, in a strange way, enhanced. It made one realise that human personality is not so exclusively expressed in the face as one is apt to suppose. The posture and rhythm of each figure remained entirely characteristic; and the expressionless quality of the mask emphasised all other means of expression. Incidentally, we found that those immobile masks gave to a listening figure an intensity which more mobile features never seem to achieve.

Of course, it is not suggested that masks would be suitable for the kind of acting in which subtle and constantly changing shades of expression are required—such acting as is called for by the plays of Shakespeare or of Chekhov—but where a powerful simplicity is demanded the most obvious drawback of the mask becomes an asset.

THE DÉCOR

NOW WITH THE HEADS AND HAIR AND FACES so far removed from realism, it was out of all question that bare hands should be seen. A member of the Chorus whose face appeared to be carved out of teak or olive, whose frame, heavily padded across the shoulders, bespoke a dejected infirmity, in whose gait was seen the palsied tottering of extremist eld,[5] could hardly thrust out of his sleeves the plump pink paw of a vigorous man of thirty. The sleeves had to be looped and draped over gloves carefully but inconspicuously painted to match the dress. In more extreme cases, more extreme hands were called for. The most spectacular were for Tiresias who, it was planned, should have bird-like claws. The fact that they took on a crustaceous aspect was by the way. The old Priest was given long bony fingers which matched his ivory dome. Jocasta and Oedipus were planned in silver and gold. It was found that Oedipus needed two pairs of hands. The first, long-nailed and golden-fingered, was encrusted with gold rings; the second was ringless for the final scene when the golden mask was veiled.

Now it began to be apparent that the décor would have to have the courage of its convictions, that masked actors, some of them in shoes with soles six inches thick, would have their freedom of expression very severely limited. How would all this work?

Let us take the play step by step and endeavour to suggest some of its meanings and how we interpreted these meanings in terms of practical stagecraft.

---

[5] This phrasing is probably a reference to Shakespeare's *Measure For Measure*, Act 3, Scene 1: 'Or all thy blessed youth becomes as aged, and doth beg the alms of palsied eld.'

Design of Tiresias, by Tanya Moiseiwitsch

Conceptual design of the Priest, by Tanya Moiseiwitsch

The scene is Thebes. One deduces an entrance to the palace and access from a city which can, with symbolic advantage, be imagined below, at the foot of a rock on which the royal residence, half palace, half fortress, is founded. An alter is required: the statues of Athena, Dionysus and Apollo may be inferred. For all this, the stage at Stratford was reasonably suitable. It permitted no literal suggestion of locality but did, we thought, sufficiently suggest an entrance to a palace of no identifiable date or style. It was insufficiently large, ominous, majestic; not exactly right but not, we believed, obstructively wrong. There were excellent entrances from below, the whereabouts of Delphi and Cithaeron could be sufficiently indicated: an altar could be simply contrived. For statues of deities we had no room, nor were we anxious to juxtapose them with what we hoped would be the monumental and sculptured-looking figures of the actors. The altar was to be supposed that of Apollo. Other deities must be vaguely and not specifically addressed.

The play opens with a processional entrance of the mourning inhabitants of plague-stricken Thebes. They come to invoke, through an aged Priest who is their spokesman, the help of Oedipus in discovering the cause of the pestilence.

The suppliant citizens wore shapeless dresses of very dark grey, mottled with black and dark blue and brown; their faces were covered with flat masks of gauze, like those of a surgeon at an operation. The idea was that these figures should be totally anonymous, unidentifiable as to age, sex or stature. Four of the suppliants carried huge bowls of incense; the remaining thirty-six carried long, gaunt, pale grey branches to which were tied wisps of wool in white and grey, the traditional emblems of supplication. The Priest was a tiny figure in dead black with an emaciated bone-coloured face and very long bony fingers. The lights were very dim; from the incense bowls thick smoke curled upward. It was intended that through the smoke almost nothing should be visible but the wool-hung branches of the suppliants, some as much as eight feet high, slowly invading and surrounding the entrance to the palace.

Then the Chorus entered down stairs on either side of the palace, fifteen old men in varying tones, not pale, not dark, of earth colours—grey, sepia, umber. Then guards in black and grey with lead-coloured masks and enormously long spears. Then, last of all, alone and from the palace, Oedipus, toweringly large, in gold.

All this occurred in absolute silence, and very slowly, with the smoke from the incense wreathing and curling and obscuring all detail, so that the effect of the masks upon an unaccustomed audience was very gradual. Our hope was that by the time the King began to speak the audience might already be inclined to accept the masks, already be inclined to look for symbols, not realism, be prepared for speech that was not an imitation of 'real' conversation, but the incantation of a ritual.

The long speech by the aged Priest, which opens the play, was very skilfully delivered by the actor to establish a convention of highly stylised declamation from which no one departed all evening. But, at the same time, within this highly artificial framework, he contrived the greatest possible variety of pitch and tempo and, while making its literal meaning clear, gave the speech an overall musical shape. It was, in fact, treated as an operatic aria.[6]

At the same time, the choreography endeavoured to establish the convention of movement to which the audience would be asked to subscribe: a movement at all times governed by the music of the spoken word, a movement in which each actor expresses himself individually within an overall symphonic pattern. In the opening aria we tried to help the audience to expect movement which, while mostly very slow, would also by realistic standards be very exaggerated. For instance, instead of kneeling in supplication to the King, the Priest lay absolutely prostrate. The supporting counterpoint of choral supplication was equally broad. One gentleman, whose mask and figure suggested that he was about a hundred and ten years old, lay on his back, head downwards on the staircase. Other goings-on were no less extreme. This extremity was the inevitable consequence of the décor, which was itself so strong that merely life-sized acting would have been completely swamped.

Whether all this achieved much of its intention, one can never tell. The intention was to remove the play completely from the area of theatrical naturalism, and to compel the audience to relate what they were seeing and hearing to their religious experience; at the same time to accustom the audience to sights and sounds so unfamiliar

---

[6] The actor playing the Priest was Eric House (1921-2004), an important figure in the birth of modern Canadian theatre.

that, if unprepared, would be extremely distracting and probably get laughs. Above all, the attempt was to raise the tragedy from the triviality of detail and particularity, on to the plane where it belongs, of abstracted and remote grandeur. The exact details of the story of What Happened to Poor Mr. A. and Mrs. B. may be interesting and deeply touching, but insofar as they are just details and insofar as Mr. A. and Mrs. B. are just individuals, the story remains on the level of journalism, remains bourgeois, our interest remains on the level of gossip and the emotion aroused is not tragic but pathetic. Tragedy presupposes the abstraction of Mr. A. from Main Street, or Mrs. B. from the wash-line and the sink, and our own abstraction with them from the trivialities of day to day, from what the very word 'journalism' denotes. The performance of a tragedy must aim higher than at an audience's susceptibility to pathos. An audience will cry readily; the death of Little Willie or a pretty girl singing the sorriest rubbish will melt to tender tears the hardest-bitten men and the hardest-biting women. The emotion aroused by even a half-decent performance of a great tragedy cannot be measured in terms of chewed hankies and misted specs. The full impact of great tragedy is not immediate; it takes effect slowly. It lies in wait on the fringe of dreams. It wakes one with a start in the small hours. It can shake the confident and strengthen the weak, stop the clock, roll back the seas. It can give a new meaning to life, and an old meaning to death.

THE COURSE OF THE PLAY

FOLLOWING THE PRIEST'S SPEECH, Oedipus promises the Thebans to do all that he can to investigate the cause of the plague, and reminds them that he has already sent his wife's brother, Creon, to consult the Oracle of Apollo at Delphi.

Creon returns with the news that to heal itself of the pestilence Thebes must drive out a defiling thing. The defilement is connected with the mysterious disappearance some years before of King Laius. Laius had been the predecessor of Oedipus on the throne of Thebes. Jocasta, now wife of Oedipus, had formerly been the wife of Laius.

The scene is full of facts; it 'plants' the whole domestic and dynastic situation; it puts the audience in possession of the facts of Laius' mysterious disappearance and suggests that these facts are important. On the emotional side it establishes a situation of some tension between Oedipus and Creon. On the philosophic side it immediately establishes that the dramatist is not going to accord unqualified reverence to the Delphic oracle and the cult of Apollo. Creon's first line, 'Pain turns to pleasure, when we have set the crooked straight' is so broadly and emphatically Delphic in style that we do not doubt that the author's intention is satirical. The satire is the more marked because Creon's entrance has been so strongly prepared. The audience is keyed up to receive important and interesting news, and is then offered this caricature of Delphic utterance. Of course, Oedipus and all on the stage take it *au grand sérieux*; the audience, however, is expected to be more sceptical.

It is a point we think insufficiently stressed by commentators that Creon brings the oracle, unsupported by written confirmation, and, furthermore, that it is Creon, not Delphi, who suggest that the defilement might be connected with the disappearance of Laius. If the play were to be interpreted on a naturalistic level, like a detective story, this might well be taken as a clue to the fact that the oracle should not be regarded by Oedipus, also that Creon is not a trustworthy fellow. It is a nice point whether, in this play, Sophocles intends to suggest the tyrant which Creon later becomes. We regarded it as an irrelevant issue and tried, like Delphi, to be ambiguously vague, showing Creon neither in a sympathetic nor an unsympathetic light.

The scene was played in a rapid, business-like key, with Oedipus perplexed, anxious, and Creon confident, assured and dominant. The mask of Creon, in bronze, was meant to suggest a face cunning, watchful and inscrutable.

Left alone, the Chorus invokes Apollo, Athena and Dionysus to drive out the god of death and pestilence. This chorus we tried to make as lyrical as we could, with the voices moving gradually nearer and nearer to song and a choreography, expressive of supplication and adoration, moving gradually from individual expression towards a unified dance. The intention was to give the audience a complete change both for the eye and ear—a different feeling, different rhythm, different colour of sound, sustained and emotional melody after a scene of business-like prose, complex but slow movement after stillness. It was designed as a bridge to carry the audience from the prosaic and 'plotty' scene with Creon to a mysterious and ironic scene of ritual, the scene of Oedipus' curse on the murderer whom the audience already suspects to be himself.

When the King reappeared after this chorus, he carried a great golden sceptre ornamented with a golden trefoil. He knelt at the altar and laid his sceptre symbolically before the god during the passage where he dedicates himself to the search for the murderer. In every way the Chorus displays fear of this curse and respect and admiration of their King—not the attitude of men towards a fellowman, but a superstitious and adoring reverence mixed with cunning and fear, the attitude of men towards a powerful and capricious god. Our aim was to suggest that to the Chorus, representing ordinary citizens, this *was* a manifestation of god, of wisdom and light made manifest, about whom they felt 'In thy light shall we see light'.

Hard upon the King's curse comes the entrance of the prophet, Tiresias. The seer is blind. The apostle of the god of light is dark. Then, later, as a result of enlightenment as to his own identity, Oedipus dashes out the light of his own eyes. The symbolism of all this seemed to us to be extremely near the heart of the play's mystery. It also seemed that, just as Delphi is presented in quite a satirical light, so is the portrait of Tiresias by no means flattering. He seems to embody the soul of superstition which we all fear and of which we are all ashamed, and which, with all our shame we cannot quire dismiss.

The figure of the prophet, then, had to suggest emphatically blindness, literally obscurantism, ferocity and intransigence. He evidently inspired awe and terror not only in the Thebans but in Oedipus as well. We wanted to make a derogatory comment upon this feeling, to imply that it was superstition rather than justified reverence, by making the figure not only formidable but squalid and a little absurd.

The prophet wore white—dead white—the first time this colour appeared. His head was that of a sort of blind and featherless bird, also dead white, a great beak between two black eyeless sockets. The hair resembled feathers. The hands and the feet were slightly feathered. The hem of the dress was torn and stained. From the scraggy neck of this apparition there depended an enormous necklace of broken eggshells. We made no attempt to depict the legendary bisexuality of Tiresias but attempted only to suggest a terrifying being of incredible age who had studied, lived, loved and feared the birds so long and so deeply that at last he had become a sort of bird.

The scene with Tiresias was played with a great deal of violent movement and shouting. Tragic dignity and nobility were thrown to the winds. The prophet raved and screamed, took an epileptic fit, fell headlong down steps. The King was shown to be touched to the quick by the hints and accusations. He too screamed in a fury of fear and rage. The Chorus reacted no less violently to the abandoned and wild passions of the great ones. It was played at a galloping speed except for a heavily marked moment when Oedipus asks, 'Who was my father?' Then

James Mason as King Oedipus, Stratford, Ontario, 1954

Donald Davis as Tiresias, Stratford, Ontario, 1954

again, at the end, there was a long, slow passage of silent mime after the prophet has gone, when Oedipus for the first time realises that he *may* be defiled, that the net *may* be closing around him, and when the old men of Thebes, battered by the events of the scene, refuse to look at their King, shrink from his touch, allow him to see that the prophet's words have taken some root in their hearts. Then Oedipus withdraws, manifestly shaken to the core.

The Chorus drew together and expressed the horror of decent, conventional people confronted with something they regard as monstrous, not to be spoken of, not to be thought of. This chorus, a terse and powerful condensation of the original, is in Yeats' finest frenzy; the fifteen men who played the Chorus at Stratford performed it with extraordinary effect—a steady *crescendo* and *accelerando* from a slow whisper of fear to a rapid bellow of bourgeois hate and defiance, a really formidable exhibition of the little man at bay, the worm turning, conventional goodness baring its savage fangs.

Right on top of this, Creon entered like a clap of thunder, scattering the Chorus from the stage. The scene between Creon and Oedipus was conducted in a series of sharp *crescendos* each coming to a climax, mounting at last to full power on the invocation of Thebes and the entrance of the Queen.

Here, as again and again, it is apparent that the form of this tragedy is far nearer to opera than to the conventional 'naturalistic' play of today. This scene is a great duet for tenor and bass. What is said is only partly adequate if divorced from a more powerful musical form than 'natural' conversation.

Paradoxically, it was in the passages of stichomythia, the single line speeches, that the Yeats' version proved least adequate. The great speeches of declamation, so we thought, were effective in their stark simplicity. It was the short, sharp dialogue exchanges which lacked form. They were clear, aristocratic, but they did not chime and ring and move forward on the twin impulse, which is not only logical but musical.

It is noticeable that the anger of Oedipus with Creon is not rational. Creon speaks and behaves reasonably; Oedipus does not. The explanation offered to Jocasta, to explain his rage, is a transparently feeble rationalisation. The anger of Oedipus, we believe, arises from feelings of guilt and fear provoked by his formidable encounter with Tiresias.

The 'Commos', (or in operatic parlance, Ensemble for Principals and Chorus) which follows the quarrel between Creon and Oedipus, has been omitted by Yeats. This seemed to us to ruin an indispensable musical transition. Borrowing heavily from other translations, we put back this Ensemble, as a bridge which led from the tumult and agitation of the quarrel to the calm of the great scene of recollection between Jocasta and Oedipus.

Incidentally, this short bridge faced the Chorus with its most exacting technical problem of the performance. The final chorus lines had to be spoken *rallentando* and *diminuendo*, while at the same time each member of the Chorus moved backwards from the stage, separating himself from his fellows. It is always hard for a Chorus to keep in unison on a *rallentando* rhythm; the difficulty was immensely increased by having to separate in space, while holding together in rhythm and feeling.

OEDIPUS AND JOCASTA

OEDIPUS NOW RECALLS a series of events from his early life. In terms of dramatic construction, it may at first glance seem odd that these facts, which it is essential for the audience to hear, should be recapitulated to his wife. But, of course, this is highly significant. Jocasta must be supposed to be hearing them for the first time. Oedipus has not hitherto been able to confide these particular memories even to her. They have, to use one of the psychological technical terms which cannot in this context be avoided, been repressed. Sophocles has been at pains to suggest that the recollection is wrung out of Oedipus as the result of shock, and that it is dredged up from the depths of his being. The whole scene is a confusion, with Jocasta in the role of priest, Oedipus as penitent. It is also strikingly like a psychological analysis, with Jocasta as doctor, Oedipus as patient. There is, further, a marked suggestion of a child 'owning up' to Mother.

Although much of its detail is not relevant to the specific question of design and the visual impression of the play, nevertheless it was from consideration of this scene that our whole idea of the play's interpretation originated. The scene is so crucial to any interpretation of the play that it must be discussed in some detail. Therefore, we quote the Yeats' text:

Jocasta: In the name of the Gods, King, what put you in anger?

Oedipus: I will tell you: for I honour you more than these men do. The cause is Creon and his plots against me.

Jocasta: Speak on, if you can tell clearly how this quarrel arose.

Oedipus: He says that I am guilty of the blood of Laius.

Jocasta: On his own knowledge, or on hearsay?

Oedipus: He has made a rascal of a seer his mouthpiece.

Jocasta: Do not fear that there is truth in what he says. Listen to me, and learn to your comfort that nothing born of woman can know what is to come. I will give you proof of that. An oracle came to Laius once, I will not say from Phoebus, but from his ministers,[7] that he was doomed to die by the hand of his own child spring from him and me. When his child was but three days old, Laius bound its feet together and had it thrown by

---

[7] Phoebus was another name for the Greek god, Apollo (who was often called Phoebus Apollo). His shrine at Delphi housed the famous Oracle whose priests ('ministers') revealed to Oedipus the dreadful prophesy of his life.

sure hands upon a trackless mountain; and when Laius was murdered at the place where three highways meet, it was, or so at least the rumour says, by foreign robbers. So Apollo did not bring it about that the child should kill its father, not did Laius die in the dreadful way he feared by his child's hand. Yet that was how the message of the seers mapped out the future. Pay no attention to such things. What the God would show he will need no help to show it, but bring it to light himself.

Oedipus: What restlessness of soul, lady, has come upon me since I heard you speak, what a tumult of the mind!

Jocasta: What is this new anxiety? What has startled you?

Oedipus: You said the Laius was killed where three highways meet.

Jocasta: Yes; that was the story.

Oedipus: And where is the place?

Jocasta: In Phocis where the road divides branching off to Delphi and to Daulia.

Oedipus: And when did it happen? How many years ago?

Jocasta: News was published in this town just before you came into power.

Oedipus: O Zeus! What have you planned to do unto me?

Jocasta: He was tall; the silver had just come into his hair; and in shape not greatly unlike to you.

Oedipus: Unhappy that I am! It seems that I have laid a dreadful curse upon myself, and did not know it.

Jocasta: What do you say? I tremble when I look on you, my King.

Oedipus: And I have a misgiving that the seer can see indeed. But I will know it all more clearly, if you tell me one thing more

Jocasta: Indeed, though I tremble I will answer whatever you ask.

Oedipus: Had he but a small troop with him; or did he travel like a great man with many followers?

Jocasta: There were but five in all—one of them a herald; and there was one carriage with Laius in it.

Oedipus: Alas! It is now clear indeed. Who was it brought the news, lady?

Jocasta: A servant—the one survivor.

Oedipus: Is he by chance in the house now?

Jocasta: No; for when he found you reigning instead of Laius he besought me, his hand clasped in mine, to send him to the fields among the cattle that he might be far from the sight of this town; and I sent him. He was a worthy man for a slave and might have asked a bigger thing.

Oedipus: I would have him return to us without delay.

Jocasta: Oedipus, it is easy. But why do you ask this?

Oedipus: I fear that I have said too much, and therefore I would question him.

Jocasta: He shall come, but I too have a right to know what lies so heavy upon your heart, my King.

Oedipus: Yes: and it shall not be kept from you now that my fear has grown so heavy. Nobody is more to me than you, nobody has the same right to learn my good or evil luck. My father was Polybus of Corinth, my mother the Dorian Merope, and I was held the foremost man in all that town until a thing happened—a thing to startle a man, though not to make him angry as it made me. We were sitting at a table, and a man who had drunk too much cried out that I was not my father's son—and I, though angry, restrained my anger for that day; but the next day went to my father and my mother and questioned them. They were indignant at the taunt and that comforted me—and yet the man's words rankled, for they had spread a rumour through the town. Without consulting my father or my mother I went to Delphi, but Phoebus told me nothing of the thing for which I came, but much of other things—things of sorrow and of terror: that I should live in incest with my mother, and beget a brood that men would shudder to look upon; that I should be my father's murderer. Hearing those words I fled out of Corinth, and from that day have but known where it lies when I have found its direction by the stars. I sought where I might escape those infamous things—the doom that was laid upon me. I came in my flight to that very spot where you tell me this king perished. Now, lady, I will tell you the truth. When I had come close up to those three roads, I came upon a herald, and a man like you have described seated in a carriage. The man who held the reins and the old man himself would not give me room, but thought to force me from the path, and I struck the driver in my anger. The old man, seeing what I had done, waited till I was passing him and then struck me upon the head. I paid him back in full, for I knocked him out of the carriage with a blow of my stick. He rolled on his back, and after that I killed them all. If this stranger were indeed Laius, is there a more miserable man in the world than the man before you? Is there a man more hated of Heaven? No stranger, no citizen, may receive him into his house, not a soul may speak to him, and

> no mouth but my own mouth has laid this curse upon me. Am I not wretched? May I be swept from this world before I have endured this doom!

The shock of the Tiresias scene, then of the quarrel with Creon, is now capped for Oedipus by the dreadful intimations of Jocasta's speech about the death of Laius. 'I have a right to know,' says Jocasta, 'what lies so heavy on your heart.' 'Yes,' Oedipus replies, 'and it shall not be kept from you now that my fear has grown so heavy.' The reiterated 'heavy' is Yeats, not Sophocles. It is indicative that Yeats too saw this as a confessional scene, saw Oedipus as a penitent longing to shed a heavy load of guilt.

Again, when halfway through the great speech, Oedipus approaches the hard core of his repression, he says, 'Now, lady, I will tell you the truth.' Does not this suggest that between the husband and wife there had been not merely concealment but prevarication?

Next notice how many of the incidentals of the story are symbolic. The detail is not mere decoration to make the story more picturesque. It is very carefully and consciously selected to set certain ideas in train by the power of association. Now it is obviously a mistake to try and label a symbol with a precise or definitive meaning. If the author wished to be precise or definitive he would not be using symbols. Nevertheless, it may be of some interest to suggest some of the possible symbolic associations attached to some of the details of the encounter of Oedipus and Laius, provided it is always understood that such associations and their interpretation are essentially subjective. Each of us is entitled to make his own interpretation. By speaking symbolically and not in direct matter-of-fact tones the author deliberately asks each interpreter to use his own imagination.

We quote our own interpretation, therefore, not as being in any sense authoritative, but simply because the interpretation of this remarkable series of symbols led us to conclusions about the meaning of the play, and thence to practical decisions in the matter of production.

First, Oedipus is speaking. He is the 'I' of the narrative. The symbols are presented as occurring to his consciousness. Nevertheless Oedipus is himself a symbolic figure. He stands, we believe, for Man in general, for each one of us in particular. Therefore, in interpreting the symbols of the scene we must think not only, what might this or that represent to Oedipus? but rather, what does this or that represent to me?

The dominant figure in this murder story is its victim—Laius, the Father. Here let us momentarily diverge to reflect how the figure of the Murdered Father haunted the consciousness and the sub-consciousness of Shakespeare. The Murdered Father dominates *Hamlet*; the Murdered King who is a symbolic father of his subjects, or, in psychological parlance, a father figure, dominates *Macbeth*, dominates *Julius Caesar*. While Lear is not literally murdered by Regan and Goneril, he is a figure of the Destroyed Father—it is parricide at one remove.

Now let us consider how Sophocles presents this father figure. He is described: tall, like Oedipus in shape, his hair beginning to whiten. Compare the description of Hamlet's father: 'his beard a sable silvered'. The intention evidently is to present a majestic figure, not young, but not old, and to insist on the likeness to Oedipus, the likeness to the 'I' of the story.

The emphasis upon Laius is the more marked because of the complete lack of emphasis upon the adoptive parents Polybus and Merope. They are presented without character of any kind.

Corinth is presented without detail except that the rumour which alarmed Oedipus was provoked by the drunken man at a feast. Is not this episode intended to exemplify the great part played by chance or luck, or even by Apollo, in human affairs? If it had not been for a chance word by a babbling drunkard thrown by chance in his way, Oedipus need never have known he was not the real son of Polybus and Merope. Unlucky chance, or a calculating predestinating Apollo, brought him face to face with Laius at a narrow pass, took him to Thebes of all the many cities he might have gone to, taught him the lucky answer to the Sphinx, rewarded him with the hand of Jocasta.

After learning he was not the son of the ruler of Corinth, Oedipus sought advice from Delphi. The answer, that he would kill his real father and be husband to his real mother, was so shocking that he fled from Delphi by night, in a darkness symbolic of terror, mystery, confusion and immensity. Corinth thereafter was but an image, discernible by starlight—no longer ever to be in the rational, daylit, everyday world.

'Now, lady, I will tell you the truth.' And here suddenly the matter of whereabouts becomes significant and symbolic—a crossroads, a crux, a place of decision. It was at a crossroads, and with some of the same symbolic overtones, that Peer Gynt met Destiny in the person of Button Moulder.

Sophocles has been at pains to 'plant' the importance of this place where three ways meet. It is repeatedly mentioned. The ways divide to Delphi and to Daulia. Delphi would seem to suggest what many psychologists believe the Left Hand, movements or turnings to the left, implies in dreams, a movement away from consciousness, away from rationality. Daulia, therefore, we suppose, implies a right-hand turn, in the direction of common sense.

As well, however, as being a place of decision, the place where three ways meet can also be regarded as a symbol of another kind. We asked a psychiatrist how he would interpret this symbol if it occurred in the dream of a patient. His reply, quite unbiased by the context which was not revealed to him until after he had answered the question, was this: To the primitive mind this symbol would immediately suggest the place where the trunk meets the legs, the 'fork' of the human body.

Oedipus encounters Laius, then, in a place of decision, and a place where, in physiological terms, the organs of sex are situation. The locality is further described in terms which seem to confirm the sexual symbolism. In one of the invocatory speeches at the end of the play Oedipus cries, 'O three roads, O secret glen, O coppice and narrow way where three roads met; you that drank up the blood I spilt, the blood was my own, my father's blood.' That is the Yeats version. Gilbert Murray's confirms the analogy:

'O Crossing of the Roads,

O secret glen and dusk of crowding woods,

O narrow footpath creeping to the brink where meet the Three.

I gave you blood to drink. Do ye remember?

'Twas my life-blood hot from my own father's heart.'
Sheppard translates:

'O ye three roads, O secret mountain-glen,

Trees, and a pathway narrowed to the place

Where met the three, do you remember me?

I gave you blood to drink, my father's blood,

And so my own.'

And Jebb: 'O ye three roads, and thou secret glen—thou coppice and narrow way where three paths meet—ye who drank from my hands that father's blood which was mine own.'

The evidence is hard to gainsay that the meeting of the three ways is itself an image of the meeting of the three lives of Laius, Oedipus and Jocasta, and that the physical description is a veiled but unmistakable allusion to the female anatomy.

Now notice that the father figure is described as seated in a carriage. His powers in the eyes of the son are 'extended'. Means of transport with their attributes of speed and mobility are well-known symbols of power. Every young child longs nowadays for a bicycle, where in another generation it longed for a pony. The longed-for extension once obtained, it is immediately turned in the child's imagination into a still more powerful extension of personality; the bicycle becomes an imaginary horse, or a railway engine (the iron horse of the nineteenth century), or car, or aeroplane (the winged horse of the twentieth century). And to the normal child these power-symbols are associated with its father. The kitchen, and all that therein is, belongs to Mummy, the source of nutriment and cosiness; the car, with its associations of power, speed, adventure, is Daddy's.

The fact that Laius is mounted on a carriage enhances the image of Laius as a powerful father figure. When Oedipus meets him and disputes the possession of this highly significant passage, it is not just one man meeting another. The foot passenger, though younger and therefore probably stronger, is at a tremendous disadvantage.

What are we to make of the two subsidiary figures, the two servants of Laius, one of whom is described as a 'herald'? Was he one of the five attendants upon Laius, similar to the Five-Wits of the English morality play?[8] It is possible that in earlier lost versions of the story Laius was so accompanied. In that case, one might interpret the Herald as the faculty of speech.

In the Yeats version it is made clear that Laius struck the first blow; but Yeats omits the fact that he struck with

---

[8] Five-Wits is a character in *Everyman* (1510) who personifies the five 'wits' or senses: sight, sound, touch, taste and smell. Five-Wits is a companion to Everyman, who regards him as his best friend until Five-Wits abandons him.

what Murray translates 'his iron-branched goad'[9], and Sheppard as 'his forking goad', and Jebb 'his goad with two teeth.' Sophocles makes the two men strike each other with instruments that may not unreasonably be regarded as phallic symbols. The battle is analogous to that between two stags who fight for supremacy of the herd.

Finally, Oedipus, in an access of irrational fury, not content with the destruction of Laius, kills all the servants. This suggests that in Father Murder one killing is not enough; all the attendants on the father figure must be killed as well. Compare in *Macbeth* the destruction of the two sleeping grooms in the chamber next to Duncan. The same idea occurs in *Julius Caesar* when the conspirators, in planning the murder of Caesar, wonder whether Antony must not be removed too. Antony is described as a limb of the trunk whose head is Caesar.

RELIGIOUS AND DRAMATIC RITUAL

OUR PRODUCTION WAS NOT AIMING to persuade the audience that the goings-on on the stage were really happening, not to attempt to induce illusion, but rather to make the audience participate in a ritual.

It was true, we realized, that the story of Oedipus would not be as familiar to an audience in Canada in 1954 as to an Athenian audience two thousand years earlier. But the story is extremely interesting and extremely lucidly unfolded by Sophocles. The important thing, it seemed,

---

[9] A goad is a short cane with a sharp point and crooked hook.

was that the large majority of our audience *would* be familiar with the idea of ritual re-enactment of a Saviour's Passion. It should be possible to make clear the analogy between religious and dramatic ritual, and in a manner to convince any reasonable person that the attempt was serious, respectable and untainted by sectarianism or blasphemy.

The Passion of Oedipus, we assumed, was a symbol of experiences which all human beings are compelled to undergo. To suffer with Oedipus, to partake of this Communion, the audience must be prepared to enter into a world of symbols exactly analogous to the experience of dreaming.

In dreams, the images and events of everyday are replaced by symbols arranged in patterns which do not correspond to those of everyday life. For instance, in a dream one can be simultaneously indoors and out; one can in the same dream-context encounter the living and the dead, sometimes those long dead. In a dream one can undergo astounding and terrifying experiences in perfect calm or be alarmed by apparently insignificant trifles.

Now dream-experience is subject to interpretation. It is possible by meditation and concentration, and after a little experience, to know with some degree of certainty what this or that symbol represents in terms of waking experience. In exactly analogous manner can the experience of Oedipus and the spectators' sympathetic experience when the tragedy is acted before them, be related to that of everyday.

But, just as a dream can be profoundly affecting even when uninterpreted, or misinterpreted, so we hoped, could an adequate performance of this tragedy. It might make a mysterious and even baffling impression upon many people who could not, or would not, bother to interpret its symbols. Nevertheless, the story is so strong, and corresponds to something so deep in our being, that the impression, though baffling, could hardly be negligible. Very few people, we believed, could see it without feeling that for an hour or two they had been in contact with a world no more unintelligible and far more cohesive and significant than the impression each of us constructs for himself of the real world, the world of everyday waking experience.

In terms of the stage, the scene between Oedipus and Jocasta seemed to demand stillness and concentration, the more so as it follows the *allegro agitato* of the quarrel with Creon. Oedipus stood with Jocasta's hand on his brow. The actor suggested that the long speech of recollection was delivered almost in a state of trance. When he reached the words, 'Now, lady, I will tell you the truth', he suggested, with deep and struggling breaths, a lapse into deeper trance; when the description of the murder was reached it was spoken in a fury of recollected passion. The words, 'And then I killed them all', were accompanied by a pantomime of indiscriminate violence. After that there was a long pause. The actor seemed to emerge from his trance and the speech was finished in a far calmer and more rational tone.

A BREAK IN THE ACTION

AFTER THE KING AND QUEEN WITHDREW to the palace, the Chorus gave utterance to sentiments which in Yeats's version satirizes the smugness of church-going conventionality and the attitude of those who hope by behaving well in school to deserve a handsome prize from the headmaster in the hereafter.

Regretfully we must confess that the humorous and satiric aspects, both in this chorus and elsewhere in the play, were utterly missed in this production. We were aware that this bitter humour pervades the play, even in its last tremendous lines. But we could see no way of expressing this that did not border too closely on triviality and an unseasonable flippancy. It is a confession or second-rateness. In the greatest tragedy humour is always present, just as great comedy is always shot through with sadness. An evening in the theatre of high but humourless intention is like a dinner without a sweet, meat followed by more meat and then a draught of strong and bitter coffee.

When Jocasta returns from the palace her mood is one of desperate anxiety. Gone is the former scepticism in which she bade Oedipus pay no attention to oracles and divination. The panic of Oedipus has infected her. Publicly and ceremoniously she beseeches Apollo to cleanse her city, her family and herself from pollution. Apollo, as Gilbert Murray has pointed out, means to destroy Jocasta, not to save her. Her prayer is interrupted by the arrival of the Man from Corinth, which seems like a deliverance but is really a link in the chain of destruction.

At this point—the arrival of the Man from Corinth—we broke the continuity of the play by a ten-minute intermission. Such a transgression of the author's intention was certainly not made without careful consideration. Two principal reasons governed the decision. First, the conditions of the Canadian summer and of the particular theatre for which this production was designed are such that a breath of fresh air is almost a physical necessity after about an hour in the theatre. It must be remembered that though the climate in Greece is hot too, the Dionysiac Festival occurred in the spring, not in high summer; and, more important, the audience sat in the open air. It should also be remembered that the Greek audience witnessed a performance of a familiar story in a familiar style. The audiences at Stratford were required, we believe, to make a no less stern effort of concentration and, at the same time, a considerable effort of intellectual, religious and emotional adaptation to ideas which were not in the least familiar. This led on to the second consideration: if both performers and audience were adequately to stay the course and give to the second half of the evening the same concentration as to the first, a rest and a breath of air were essential.

Why, it may be asked, should the power of endurance of a modern audience in Canada be so much less than that of an Athenian audience two thousand years ago? The question is hard to answer. The Athenian audience was predominantly local and belonged predominantly to a class of society which had plenty of help to do the bread-winning and domestic chores. One has always to bear in mind that the glory that was Greece was not achieved without the assistance of slave labour. The Athenian Festival was a great religious occasion and its audience was not only in duty and reverence bound to give its entire energies and attention to the performance, but was literally free from other and more mundane preoccupations.

In contrast, the great majority of our audience was heavily burdened by daily cares—office appointments, feeding of stock, baby-sitting and the like. Many had come a long journey and would have another long journey after the performance before they got to their beds. Above all, our performance was being given in a locality and an epoch which had entirely lost the tradition of regarding Art in general, or the Theatre in particular, as being in the realm of religion or even as being 'serious'.

The modern theatre has traditionally become associated only with entertainment. What goes on there is most usually and most indicatively described as a 'show'. Many serious and intelligent people consider that a theatrical performance can only be frivolous and is almost certain to be licentious as well. Moreover, our performance was being offered for sale commercially. The artistic intention certainly was serious and certainly was religious. But the fact remains that the priests and acolytes were being quite well paid for their services, and the members of the congregation were expected to cough up a substantial price for the privilege of attendance. In these circumstances the comfort and convenience of the audience had to have a higher consideration than if the occasion had been in every sense a religious festival, and the routine of the performance simply had to conform in certain respects to current commercial practice.

One of these respects which was felt to matter a great deal was the length of the performance. It is generally expected that the public will be entertained for a space of time that varies between two and three hours. It may seem very silly that this should be important. But if a play lasts for more than three hours, people get tired and fussed about late transport or being late to bed. If it lasts less than two hours and a half, they feel cheated of their money's worth.

The *Oedipus* of Sophocles, in our production, lasts ninety minutes. We knew very well that if our audience had been offered a performance as brief as this, no matter what the quality, it would have felt extremely dissatisfied. So, in addition to other more serious, more practical and more respectable reasons, an intermission was required to pad out the performance to a length more in conformity with the current practice of show business.

The practical problem, then, was how to affect this intermission with the least damage to the dignity and continuity of the tragedy.

By the end of Jocasta's prayer, the Queen, her attendant and all the Chorus were on their knees. Unseen by the audience, at the head of one of the aisles of the theatre, the Man from Corinth gave a great and cheerful cry of 'News! Good news!' All on the stage turned, surprised and expectant, towards the source of the cry. And then, as they rose from their knees, the stage-lights dimmed. Under cover of a moment of darkness, the actors left the stage. When the houselights came on, it was empty.

Then, at the end of the intermission, the houselights went out and, in the darkness, the actors again took up their stations, not, however, at the same place they had reached before the intermission. When the stage-lights came on they were in position to speak the chorus which follows the confession of Oedipus. Jocasta made her entrance again. The prayer was made again. But this time, after the cry of 'News', the Man from Corinth came down the aisle, was welcomed by the Chorus, led to the Queen, and the play proceeded.

By this means the second part of the play got off to a flying start. Actors and audience were given the moment of recapitulation to re-establish contact, re-establish something of the impetus which the first part of the play had generated.

The device did not entirely heal the gaping wound made by the intermission in the play's continuity; but it did at least suggest that a feeling of continuity was being sought. In practical terms it means that the audience had time to 'settle' before the Man from Corinth began his scene, before there was new material to assimilate.

The Corinthian had a round, jolly, smiling, simpleton's face; in size and texture his mask resembled those of the Chorus. To show that he had made a journey, that he was an outsider, he carried a powerful staff and had a big hat slung on his back. He was played as a hearty, countrified fellow, quite unaware, until too late, of the deadly nature of his news.

Tony Van Bridge as the Man from Corinth, costume and masks designed by Tanya Moiseiwitsch and Jacqueline Cundall

William Needles as the Old Shepherd, Stratford, Ontario, 1954

THE SECOND PART

WHEN OEDIPUS RETURNED, he crept on to the stage furtively, fearfully, in strong contrast to the royal and confident manner of earlier entrances. For a moment the news of the death of Polybus seems to promise relief, then suddenly fear is only further confirmed and it begins to look likely that he has not only murdered his father but that the other and even more horrible prediction of the oracle is about to be fulfilled, that he is living as his mother's husband.

To Jocasta the frightful truth is inescapable. The anguish of her realisation is one of the great moments of the play, of all drama. The refusal by Oedipus to recognize the depth of this anguish, his pretence that it is merely an outburst of petulant dynastic pride by Jocasta is extremely hard to accept. It is only possible to make it plausible if it is part of the wild exaltation which now takes hold of the King, and which expresses powerfully the way human consciousness refuses to face a reality which is too unpleasant to be borne, until the confrontation is entirely inevitable.

This passage, in which Oedipus, flying from reality, takes refuge in the fantastic notion that he is the child of Good Luck, is one of the greatest of many great strokes of insight in the play. Just so, we are led to believe, did Hitler behave in the last phase. Reality is too terrible to contemplate; fear must be compensated by the fantasy of an imaginary identity more splendid than the real one, and an easy and agreeable future arranged by Destiny—a mother figure.

In a kind of delirium, utterly unable to face the idea of his real mother's identity, Oedipus invokes a fictious and supernatural mother. In the same breath that he upbraids Jocasta for dynastic pride, he is claiming kinship with the years, with the months. The years, be it noted, are periods of time measured by the number of revolutions the sun makes around the earth; the moon shines only in the light of the sun god. All this new-claimed kindred of Oedipus have in common is their dependence upon the sun. All unawares Oedipus is asserting his kinship with that very sun god who is about to destroy him.

At the same time, the Chorus of Thebans catch the exaltation of their King. They to turn to a mother figure but not, like Oedipus, to Good Luck or to Deity. The Thebans turn to Cithaeron, the mountain which dominates their city. It is often the case that a landmark, natural or man-made, acquires great symbolic importance and a personality like that of an older friend or a substitute parent. To thousands of Londoners during the air-raids of 1940-45, St. Paul's Cathedral became a symbol, a personalization of Mother London, and the voice of Big Ben proclaiming the hours so regularly, in a tone so constant, so reliable, so familiar, was the voice of a dear and greatly respected elder brother.

So now in this strange and irrational moment of excitement, the Thebans invoke Mount Cithaeron. Oedipus, whom hitherto they had regarded as a great man, almost a god, but a foreigner, is now revealed as one of

Theban origin, one of themselves. Infected by his ecstasy, they hail the mother-mountain; they praise Oedipus as the son of one of the mountain-nymphs begotten in a hidden glen (a striking reiteration of the glen image) of Cithaeron by Pan, Apollo or Dionysus.

The feeling of this chorus is ecstatic. It is a raising of Oedipus to the heights before he is dashed into the abyss. It is a moment analogous to the time in a sacrifice when the victim is crowned with garlands just before the knife is placed across its throat. It is the ride to Jerusalem on Palm Sunday.

We endeavoured to make this chorus extremely primitive. There was chanting, stamping, much fawning and flopping before Oedipus. The chorus itself was very softly spoken, moving imperceptibly from speech to the sustained melodic line of a two-part chorale which faded again back into speech and thence to silence. Oedipus stood with raised arms and uplifted head in the centre of a cluster of prostrate adorers. The group was held for a moment motionless and silent. Then Oedipus, turning his head, lowering his arms, seemed to feel the approach of the Old Shepherd.

The Old Shepherd was a tiny, bowed figure. His face was round and wrinkled and dark, sunburned to a deep mahogany. The head was covered with little white woolly curls and, over his shoulders, was a white woolly cape. He was led by two guards very, very slowly down a long aisle to the stage. When he approached the stage the old men of the Chorus surrounded him in silence and he was lifted very gently and slowly and deposited in front of the King.

The movement was not in the least realistic, but it did, we think, powerfully and movingly, present this confrontation of Oedipus with his Destiny, in the form of this tiny, bowed and trembling figure. The brief and terrible scene of question and answer between King and Shepherd was played very quietly, with no theatrical fireworks, no climax.

Finally, face to face with irrefutable proof of his identity and his guilt, the King paused a short while. There was a hush in every audience who saw the play that was like the deathly stillness before thunder. Then with a low moan he acknowledged his own accursedness, took farewell of the light, and withdrew into the shadows of the palace. In fading light, the Chorus mourned for him.

In an endeavour to make this an entirely ritualistic expression and to remove it from the particularity of private grief, it was spoken in unison, rather as the prayers are chanted in a High Anglican liturgy, by tenors and basses antiphonally. The grouping was no less formal. This did, we think, give it an effect primarily musical and only secondarily emotional. The audience had been asked to share a long spell of emotional tension. This chorus must provide a rest without breaking the mood, must voice the audience's pity, but must do so formally, gravely, without tears or passion. It must be a quiet bridge from the catastrophe to the Messenger's narration of violence and horror. By the end of the chorus the stage was nearly dark. The figures were no more than mourning, chanting shadows.

The Messenger was heard, rather than seen, to emerge from the palace, clinging to the walls, clutching at the pillars, an entirely black figure with a contorted mask of grief and horror coloured like pewter or lead. His narration describes the suicide of Jocasta, the discovery of her body by Oedipus, and how he blinds himself. As in the scene between Jocasta and Oedipus which we have considered at length, the details of this speech are all symbolic, all have a second meaning. We do not propose to discuss them. They confirmed us in our opinion that the play must be symbolically and not literally interpreted; but nothing that is said here affected the visual scheme.

THE USE OF LIGHTING

IT HAS BEEN A MATTER of some concern to us how far to use light on the Stratford stage as a decoration and a means of enhancing atmosphere, as opposed to a merely utilitarian source of illumination.

It has always been our view that one should not be doctrinaire or dogmatic, partly because dogmatism is never a good idea, and partly because doctrines can, on this topic, reach opposing conclusions. It is possible to maintain that an apron-stage and an auditorium in arena form are denials of the idea of theatrical illusion and that, therefore, lighting must not be used for illusionary purposes. But is seems to us that 'fancy' lighting need not necessarily have an illusionary purpose. It can be used, for instance, to place emphasis here or there on the stage, or for purely decorative purposes, or as an aid to atmosphere, even if only by the cliché method of bright light for cheerful scenes, dim light for scenes which are melancholy or mysterious. To use dim light to suggest evening, however, seems to us the wrong, the illusionary idea. Partly through being in doubt about this, partly, let us admit, because the lighting plant at Stratford is rather inexpensive and therefore rather inflexible, we have hitherto confined ourselves to nothing more elaborate than an occasional unobtrusive dimming or checking of light on certain occasions when it seemed appropriate—the romantic finales, for instance, in Shakespearean comedy, the battle scenes in *Richard III* and *Julius Caesar*, the prison scenes in *Measure for Measure*.

The final scenes of *Oedipus* were played in a considerable degree of dimness for several purposes: first, for the rather obvious reason of enhancing a romantic and therefore probably inappropriate and over-sentimental atmosphere of melancholy; second, and more defensibly, as a symbol of the spiritual darkness descending upon Thebes and the physical blindness descending upon the King; third, to mark visually as well as musically the fact that the catastrophe of the play is succeeded by a long declining movement, a quiet *decrescendo*. Finally, there was the practical consideration that the visual detail of Oedipus' blinding must not be realistic but that we had not quite sufficient confidence in our stylistic solution of this problem to expose it to harsh light and detailed scrutiny.

We had both seen this blindness realistically suggested. Laurence Olivier had played the part with deserved and immense acclaim. But when he re-entered for this final scene festooned with plastic streams of crimson lake, which elaborately attempted, but utterly failed, to suggest rivers of blood pouring from ruined sockets, we had both felt that the attempt was mistaken not only in practice but in theory. It was exposing what had been deliberately concealed by the author from the sight of the audience; it was doing again what had been done better in the words of the Messenger. By forcing the audience's attention, but not its conviction, upon the material details of the blinding, it was detracting attention from the spiritual meaning. An incomplete and unsuccessful realistic effect was replacing the immeasurably greater imaginative possibility of a symbol.

How was this symbolic effect to be achieved?

We cannot tell whether or not our attempt was satisfactory. It certainly had one merit: extreme simplicity. The King wore an immense and shapeless robe of dark purplish crimson, in thick woollen material. The head and face were covered with a thick veil of black fishing net. By this means there would be, we hoped, an indirect association, through colour, with blood; the ruined face and head were concealed but in such a way that the actor could see, that his speech would not be muffled; and, not least important with a long and exacting scene to play, he could take deep and unimpeded breaths.

THE LAST SCENE

THE FINAL SCENE, with its long and apparently, self-pitying expressions of grief, its long recapitulation of Oedipus' misdeeds like one of the public confessions in Dostoevsky, its long insistence upon funerary formalities, its long dwelling upon the unfortunate position of the daughters—all this is very far removed from the sort of attitude to disaster which we now expect a hero to show. There is none of the decent reticence, the stiff upper lip which in contemporary Western society is expected of a soldier and a gentleman. There is no Christian resignation and little Christian fortitude. There is nothing of that much-admired attitude of a bloodhound by Landseer— faithful, red-rimmed doggy eyes turned trustingly upwards towards a kind master. But then Apollo has not been shown as a kind master, a benign father, a wise counsellor or reliable friend. It is questionable if the Deity has been shown in even so sympathetic a light as a remote and disinterested force. The trusting upward gaze could only seem in the context either hypocritical or idiotic.

Perhaps the hardest thing of all to apprehend is the long-drawn lament over the children. In realistic terms one is irritated by its selfishness and tactlessness. Daddy is making things so much worse for the poor dears. And, anyway, haven't we all known children to survive a disastrous start in life? They are young enough to begin a new life in a totally different environment with a placid, kind adopted Auntie who will have enough sense to ask no awkward questions. But all such ideas are trivial and irrelevant and provincial. They assume that Greek manners are, or ought to be, the same as ours. They fail to assume the preconceptions of the audience for whom the play was written. This family, to the Athenian audience, was clearly and irrevocably doomed and polluted. There was absolutely no possibility for a new and happier life for

Ismene and Antigone. Their fate was part of the symbolic curse hanging over their symbolically polluted house.

But surely one may legitimately wonder why there should be such an amount of horror over a parricide which, in rational terms, was obviously accidental. Certainly, Oedipus was morally to blame for killing Laius, and even more so for killing his servants. But in terms of modern justice there would be more than a chance of a verdict not of murder but of manslaughter. The crime was not premeditated and there was evidence of considerable provocation. Equally, the horror over the incest seems to be excessive, if regarded rationally.

This is not the place for a general discussion on the propriety of our contemporary moral and judicial attitude to incest. It would appear to be a crime which is regarded in contemporary society with a remarkably primitive degree of horror and blame, surrounded by secrecy and superstition, removed by tacit and almost universal agreement from the realm of rational consideration. But since the incest of Oedipus and Jocasta was committed entirely unwittingly there can, in their case, be no question of blame or guilt or shame. The horror is not a particular one arraigning these two guilty individuals. It is an expression of horror at the idea of incest of general. It is presented in this play as one of the ultimates in Pollution.

THE FREUDIAN INTERPRETATION

NOW, CLEARLY, if the play is rightly to be regarded as we regard it, as an allegory, a series of symbolic events occurring to symbolic persons in symbolic environments, then any intelligent person must wonder how to interpret not only such subsidiary symbols as Laius' carriage, the meeting of three ways, Jocasta's self-slaughter by hanging or Oedipus dashing in the doors of her marriage-chamber which was also her death-chamber. It is even more important, and far harder, to find the meaning of the three or four great symbolic themes round which the tragedy is constructed—pollution, parricide, incest, blindness or darkness, contrasted with light. Perhaps the most important and the most baffling symbol of all is Apollo.

Here, of course, is the place where it would be great to come out with a notable discovery, to utter the last irrefutable word, to confound previous critics and amaze those yet unborn, to interpret satisfyingly, completely, once and for all, this majestic and fascinating enigma.

But even for the interpretation of riddles Sophocles offers a rather ominous symbol. The Sphinx propounded a riddle. Oedipus supplied the answer. It is true that this delivered Thebes from the Sphinx, who dived off a rock and never was seen again. But for Thebes, Sphinx was succeeded by pestilence. And just look what happened to Oedipus!

In our epoch it is quite hard to look for our solution in other than Freudian terms. Freud has revolutionized our conception of ourselves, and one of the pillars of the Freudian edifice is the Oedipus complex. It is all too easy to think because of its topicality that this is what the tragedy is about; and certainly it is one of the themes. But surely the relation of Oedipus to Jocasta and Laius is far less important than his relation to Apollo. The tragedy is about Man and God and only secondarily about Child and Parent. In other words, psychology must not, in our view, be allowed to overshadow theology.

It is noticeable that the father-son relation, though important to the play, is never applied to the connection of Apollo with mortals. Apollo is never presented as a father figure, nor is any mention made of a father god, a conception which was as familiar to the Greeks as to the Jews or to ourselves or to any patriarchal society.

It is true that under stress of great emotion, as we have seen, Oedipus does appeal to a fictitious mother goddess, Good Luck or Chance. Incidentally, is it intended that at this moment he appeals to a deity who is traditionally represented as blind? There is, however, no suggestion whatever that this particular speech represents any serious theological idea, on the part of either Oedipus or Sophocles.

Therefore, while our opinion is anything but definite, and can only be advanced with great diffidence, we think that theologically the symbolism of the play does not relate God to Man as a parent; it suggests the Immanence of God in Man, or perhaps, more widely and vaguely, the Immanence of God in Nature.

There is, we suggest, a strong and repeated suggestion of scepticism about priesthood and oracles. Tiresias, although right in what he says about Oedipus, is not a sympathetic portrait; the scene greatly misses irony unless he is presented as a disreputable kind of fakir. Again, the pronouncement which Creon brings from Delphi at the beginning of the play, and the Delphic prophecies first to Laius and then to Oedipus, which had been made before the events of the play, all turn out to be true, but so confusedly and unhelpfully uttered that, in point of fact, instead of preventing they precipitate the havoc. Delphi, in short, like Tiresias, is presented unsympathetically.

It used to be almost a commonplace, when the religious implications of this play were discussed, to say that Apollo was punishing Oedipus for ὕβρις [hubris], for uppishness, for not knowing his place in the universe. This argument would be more impressive if there were more evidence of the uppishness of Oedipus. But, on the evidence of this play, he behaves with exemplary piety and humility towards Apollo, exemplary justice and humanity as a monarch. His conduct as a husband and father cannot be faulted. It is true that he is rude to Tiresias, and to Creon he is both unreasonable and unkind. But these offences are both rather lapses of manners than of morals and are committed, the first under stress of great provocation by Tiresias, the second under the stress of great perturbation. The sum of the two offences seems entirely insufficient to weigh in the scale of justice against the frightful punishments which they are supposed to have earned. Moreover, this simple moral explanation of the story derives from its facts, and not at all from the symbols with which we have been concerned.

The symbolism seems to suggest that the play certainly is concerned with Man's search for his own identity, largely in terms of 'Who is my father? Who is my mother?' But it is also no less concerned with the questions 'Who is responsible? Who is answerable?'

Implicitly, by disparaging Tiresias and Delphi, Sophocles rejects a simple childlike dependence upon a God outside ourselves. Yet, when the Leader of the Chorus directly asks Oedipus who is responsible for the terrible act of self-blinding, the answer, without apparent bitterness, without passion, is categorical: 'It is Apollo.' And at an earlier point in the play Oedipus cries, 'O God, what have you planned to do to me?' Oedipus, we must suppose, did believe that there was a power outside himself which was executing a prearranged plan.

But are we on this account to believe that Sophocles felt the same? It is a common mistake of criticism to think that a dramatic author necessarily puts his own beliefs into the mouths of his creatures. His own beliefs are implicit rather than explicit in his work.

In this play, we believe, Sophocles expresses his own beliefs not at all on the factual, literal plane, but through a language of symbols. While Oedipus is Everyman, nevertheless obviously Everyman does not murder his father and live as his mother's husband. The parricide and the incest are, as every student of Freud believes, symbols of attachment of sons to their mothers, with a consequent jealousy and hostility to their fathers. That this attachment and this hostility of Oedipus were connected with persons whom he did not know to be his father and mother, symbolizes the fact that these emotions are not conscious.

But the parricide and the incest are only two, and not necessarily the two most important, as they are certainly not the two most emphatically or frequently stated symbols in this play. We consider that the symbols of light-darkness dominate the play. And we consider that this must be interpreted as sight-blindness and thence insight-ignorance. We also consider that the connection between Apollo and Light is inescapable and that it is highly significant that this particular deity dominates the play, is related explicitly to every twist and turn of the plot and is explicitly acknowledged by Oedipus as the planner and executor of his fate.

We do not feel able to do more than draw attention to the dominance of the light-darkness motif, and to hazard the speculation—no more—that interpretation may be sought in connection with the doctrine of immanent deity, the light within ourselves.

More and more as we worked on the play, as in rehearsal we lived in it, absorbing it not so much rationally or even emotionally, but as a pianist absorbs music which has to be practised over and over and over, we became convinced that the conflict in the play was between Oedipus and Immanent Apollo, God within himself.

The tragedy would in that case, like Hamlet, be a tragedy of self-conflict. Oedipus, like Hamlet, is from beginning to end the focus of attention, is carefully, elaborately and sympathetically presented as a 'character'. But he does not consciously guide the events of the tragedy. A situation is postulated, in both *Hamlet* and *Oedipus*; it concerns a murdered father. But in both cases, though the central character acts with extraordinary intelligence, consistency and vigour (the notion that Hamlet cannot take action simply is not supported by the evidence of the play), nevertheless his decisions are all forced upon him against his conscious inclination. He is swept to destruction upon a tide of predestination.

In *Oedipus* the problem, we suggest, is how to relate the plot-motifs of parricide and incest to the philosophy which finds expression in the complex of ideas symbolized by Apollo.

God within ourselves implies that each individual has some responsibility for his own actions. Parents—the 'second parties' in the motif of parricide-incest—are also connected with the idea of responsibility. At some period the responsible man must take over the control of his own life from his father, must, in symbolic terms, smite Laius from his chariot; and at some period he must be confronted with the incestuous implications of his relation to his mother.

Can it be that the main theme of the play is the emergence of man from darkness to light by the assumption of responsibilities which in darker or more primitive stages of development are delegated to 'outside authorities—parents and non-immanent gods?

A LITERAL INTERPRETATION NOT ENOUGH

NOW BACK TO PRACTICAL MATTERS of production: Working at the last scenes of the play with two differently gifted but serious and intelligent actors, we have come to the confident conclusion that a mere literal following of the lines is not the clue to the interpretation.

It is apparent that the first speeches with the Chorus after the blinding have some further implication than self-pity and mourning. There is, we all felt, a sense of exaltation as well as of suffering. Perhaps there is something analogous to the glory of expiation upon which Roman Catholic hagiology insists. Certainly, the actor here must try to catch the note not of self-pity but of rapt exaltation.

Then comes the invocation recalling Cithaeron, Corinth, the three roads, the secret glen, the narrow way and, later in the same speech, the marriage bed. It will, we think, have been apparent that the drift of the speech was ritualistic, was a ceremonial recapitulation of crucial events in his life, a ceremonial invocation of the localities with which these events were connected. The conjunction of these words with gestures of washing may perhaps have suggested to a few spectators that this, like Lady Macbeth's handwashing, like the ritual bath in Caesar's blood, like Christian baptism, was a ceremony of purification. The idea of purification by blood is not exclusively pagan. The well-known hymn by William Cowper[10] strikingly relates it to Christian practice:

> There is a fountain filled with blood,
> Drawn from Emmanuel's veins,
> And sinners plunged beneath that flood
> Lose all their guilty stains.

---

[10] William Cowper (1731-1800) was one of most popular English poets and hymnwriters of the eighteenth century.

When Creon entered, he was accompanied by armed guards, wore the crown and carried the sceptre formerly used by Oedipus, and suggested by his demeanour that he was in the presence of an unclean and polluted thing.

The children wore sad, flat little masks and long shapeless robes in two shades of crimson. When they joined Oedipus the three figures merged into one single three-shaded crimson mass, and his speech to them deploring their fate was accompanied by a slow, tangling, weaving dance. This was again to insist upon the ritual, rather than realistic, nature of the speech, and to suggest the oneness of the three. The girls moved as if tied to their father; they were three trunks growing out of one twisted, tortured root.

At the end the children were torn from him by guards—a slow, heavy moment, one child dragged, the other lifted into the air, slowly, slowly and in silence. Then Creon withdrew.

Oedipus was alone on the stage, the Chorus hidden in the shadows. Very slowly Oedipus withdrew from the lighted area, down the steps, down a slope, always downward, out of sight. As he moved from the sight of the audience the Chorus slowly mounted the steps into the dim light of the stage and, standing motionless, monumental, spoke very simply and quietly and unemotionally the five terse powerful lines which are Yeats' version of the final chorus.

THIS ESSAY WILL CLOSE as it began with a word of apology that our scholarship is not more adequate to the task of interpreting this masterpiece and of hope that to some few readers it may be of interest to possess a record of the way a production is prepared. When a building is erected, there must first be a scaffolding to support the workmen. So, in the production of a play those who put it together in rehearsal must be supported on a previously erected scaffolding of theory and meditation translated into practical plans.

It is such a scaffolding that we have here endeavoured to describe.

CAST OF *KING OEDIPUS*, 1954

OEDIPUS REX by SOPHOCLES

In a version by W. B. Yeats

(Characters in order of their appearance)

OEDIPUS	James Mason
PRIEST	Eric House
CREON	Robert Goodier
TIRESIAS	Donald David
JOCASTA	Eleanor Stuart
MAN FROM CORINTH	Douglas Campbell
OLD SHEPHERD	William Needles
MESSENGER	Douglas Rain
CHORUS LEADER	William Hutt

CHORUS: Robert Christie, Donald Harron, Peter Mews, Bruno Gerussi, Grant Reddick, Roland Bull, Neil Vipond, Neil Carson, Jonathan White, James Manser, Edward Holmes, Bruce Swerdfager, William Shatner, Roland Hewgill

NURSE	Marionne Johnston
ISMENE & ANTIGONE, daughters of Oedipus	Lois Shaw and Valentina de Bruin

ATTENDANTS ON CREON: Warwick Butt, Vincent Edward, Jon Granik, Jack Hutt, Jim Jorgensen, John Northmore, Orest Ulan, Beverly Wilson

SUPPLIANTS: Aimé Aunapuu, Elizabeth Barry, Barbara Colley, Beatrice Dabba, Isobel Dickson, Carole Ernest, Marilyn Ernest, June Faibish, Pauline Galbraith, Dawn Greenhalgh, Olga Landiak, Margaret Hall, Jo Hutchings, Doreen Jackson, Patricia Powers, Edna Pozer, Anne Pritchard, Marie Shackleton, Rose May Sowby, Lucille Walker, Mary Warren, Joan Watts, Lynn Wilson, Sandra Wilson, Helene Winston, Charles Allen, Bob Barr, Robin Freeman, Don Gollan, John Mair, Walter Mills, Newman O'Leary, La Verne Palmier, Kenneth Pauli, Clarence Wilson, Donal Wilson

DIRECTED BY TYRONE GUTHRIE

DESIGNED BY TANYA MOISEIWITSCH

MUSIC BY CEDRIC THORPE DAVIE

Masks designed by Tanya Moiseiwitsch and Jacqueline Cundall

INTERVIEW WITH TANYA MOISEIWITSCH AND COLIN GEORGE, MAY 2001

Colin George was the first Artistic Director of the Crucible Theatre (1971-74). The Crucible's thrust stage was inspired by Tyrone Guthrie, who in 1967 arranged for George to visit the thrust stages at Stratford, Ontario and at the Guthrie Theater, Minneapolis, where he saw Guthrie and Tanya's spell-binding production of *The House of Atreus*. With Guthrie's support, Tanya was brought on board to design a new thrust stage in Sheffield. Her design drew on her previous experience in North America, but also introduced several innovations (for example, putting backstage under the stage, accessed by her trademark tunnels or vomitories at the front corners of the stage).

After the Crucible opened in November 1971, Tanya stayed on as Design Consultant (or 'Queen of Design' as George designated her), designing several productions, including his production of *The Persians* in October 1972. Six years later, she designed George's productions of *Oedipus the King* and *Oedipus at Colonus* for the Adelaide State Theatre Company, which was their last theatrical collaboration.

The following transcript is taken from Colin George's interview with Tanya at her flat in Chelsea in May 2001.

Colin: Tanya, you started working on the proscenium stage. When did you first become aware of the open stage?

Tanya: Tyrone Guthrie. He made a point of telling me if I wanted to, I could go to Canada with him and some other people and start a theatre, where they didn't have anything, it was just a hole in the ground—well, it wasn't even that. And his idea was to reproduce the best qualities of the Assembly Hall, Edinburgh which was adapted for a production that he did, but I never saw—I saw it later, but I didn't see it then—*The Thrie Estaits*. But it was kind of revolutionary, I think—but who knows what came before? They all stepped in each other's shoes. Guthrie had a way of making things happen like they never happened before. Well, I fell for that!

Colin: Had you not seen a thrust stage production before you designed Stratford? Had you been to the Assembly Hall?

Tanya: No, I hadn't. I saw photographs. And Guthrie showed me how the steps there were very steep because they had to build the stage over the Moderator's throne which they weren't allowed to stick things into. And, therefore, to get from the stage level down to the floor level and whiz off up

The Thrie Estaits *at the Assembly Hall, Edinburgh, 1948*

the aisles—the steps were very high and the women in the company complained a lot. So, he said, 'Now we're starting from scratch we can do what we like. Just see to it that the steps are much shallower, but they mustn't be so shallow that they aren't useful for people to be masked and unmasked. If you want to get rid of someone, get them down a step or two, but you don't want them to sit down or crouch, but they should leave they eyeline clear.'

And I got all of these instructions more or less on the back of an envelope—and off we went!

Colin: What are the concepts and ideas behind the open stage as you call it, not a thrust stage? If you had to say to a designer who is going to design at Stratford—what advice would you give them?

Tanya: Well, the idea was that scenery was not necessary. You went up there and did your play, but you didn't have to have any scenery, as it were, and certainly not painted scenery. It was this kind of 'Wooden O' which in itself had entrances and exits galore, you could change the shape of it just by moving your actors around. And if you wanted some sort of seating arrangement, somebody might bring on a stool or a chair, but nothing elaborate and nothing that got in the way of a quick change from one scene to another, which would run into it—indeed sometimes overlap, the next one would start before the present one had finished—and that meant you get through the plays rather more quickly. Not perhaps just "two hours traffic", as we were told by Shakespeare you could do, but it was a great speedy arrangement and they came and went at the double. Most of them were young enough to do that. The older ones of necessity went off in a more dignified way—or came on.

But I don't recall. I didn't go to rehearsals because we were always having either fittings or just making things. All of our hands were very active and our poor little brains were being overworked. Two plays, only two, going on back-to-back: *Richard III* and *All's Well That Ends Well*. Very different staging and modern dress—Guthrie's idea of 'modern dress' was rather Edwardian, you realise.

Colin: Where did the tunnels come from? Or the vomitories, I know you don't like that word.

Tanya: An awful word. They were a way of getting away quickly.

Colin: Did they come from Edinburgh?

Tanya: Well, in a way. But I think in Edinburgh it was more about the aisles and going up steps.

Colin: When it came to building the Crucible, the tunnels were very much you and Guthrie.

Tanya: Well, the going down exit was a good way out. You get rid of people very quickly. And, with luck, nobody stumbled or fell or screamed: "I'm in the wrong tunnel!" That once happened, but it wasn't a performance it was a rehearsal and an actor had to be rescued and pushed into the right tunnel!

Colin: And the gutter, as you say, was below the moderator's chair?

Tanya: Yes, and it was kind of No-Man's-Land, and no great scenes were played in the gutter. And with luck the actors had it their way, and not the audience putting their coats, or their box of chocolates, or their feet even, in the gutter. That was rather awkward. They had to be told not to do that.

Colin: About the upper stage behind—the triangle jutting out. That was perhaps inspired by The Globe, or was it just that you wanted a higher level?

Tanya: Guthrie just wanted an upstairs, which he built for *The Thrie Estaits*. But it was much narrower, much smaller, because those were the measurements of the actual hall. They couldn't fiddle with that. But when we had nothing to stop us, we decided that the point of the upper stage should jut out, rather than be flat which might look like a little proscenium on its own. And the jutting out bit was—if you sat there or stood there, you could be seen by every seat in the house. But once or twice people upstairs went further back and they were not visible to absolutely everybody—you might hear them shrieking or see a hat maybe or something, but they wouldn't be in focus. But the main thing was the line of sight. And the architects played along wonderfully with that concept.

Two views of the auditorium of the Festival Theatre, Stratford, Ontario, which replaced 'The Tent' in 1957 and which was modified in 1962.

Colin: About costuming in this sort of theatre. I know what I want you to say, should I say it for you?

Tanya: I think you may have to say it and I'll agree!

Colin: It's more three-dimensional. You said no painted scenery, you might paint the costumes. But it seemed to me the costumes were part of the scenery, and vice versa. They had a chunkiness, a three-dimensional, a sculptural quality.

Tanya: Yes, yes.

Colin: I suppose in some plays, I suppose Shakespeare was no problem, or even in *Hedda Gabler* there's no problem. But did you notice a different style in designing there—not consciously at first—from say, designing at the Abbey [Theatre, Dublin] before?

Tanya: I don't think they were related in any way. Because the Abbey was completely proscenium and very shallow—the old Abbey—a teeny-weeny stage on which they crowded endless, endless scenery and props and furniture for the '*realismus*' side of the plays that they put on. No, it had no bearing on it at all.

Colin: In terms of the Greeks, how did that emerge? *Oedipus* was the first with dear old James Mason. How did you approach that with Guthrie?

Tanya: Well, first off, Guthrie said he wanted to do it in masks, which he hadn't done before. He saw himself as an innovator in that neck of the woods. And I said: "Well, half masks. What about stopping just below the nose and the cheeks and leaving the mouth free? Make it up to look like part of the mask, but not be behind the material, whatever they were made of."

The very first year—don't ask me why—but I thought I would experiment with chamois leather and soak it in glue and stuff. It looked kind of wonderful, but I was told by the actors later in life that they got terribly hot and anything you can do to make it less hot, the whole idea of the lights and the costumes and being behind the masks—they nearly died of the heat. Because it is a very hot summer which I didn't know about.

They tried to cool it off by having blowers blowing through huge ice packs offstage, which gave people rheumatism almost, sciatica or something, and it made an awful noise, so that was right out, forget it. One or two people, they didn't actual faint, but they came off stage in very... well, shall we say, worn out condition and sort of wished perhaps they weren't there. But nobody—nobody—

complained. I think maybe they were frightened to. What would happen to them if they complained? James Mason didn't complain and if he could bear it, everyone could bear it. And as Guthrie said, "One of the handsomest men on the stage suddenly is put behind a mask. Am I mad? No, I don't think so. I think he'll talk his way out of that."

And James totally agreed with the idea. He was wonderfully gracious and a good example to everyone. And when Douglas Campbell took over the part the following year it became much more active. Dougie was a great mover around—well, they made a film of it and Dougie was in that. And that was a bit of a revelation to all of us because we didn't know it was going to be such an event.

Colin: Did you abandon the chamois leather for other materials to make the masks later? What did we do in Adelaide [for *Oedipus Rex* and *Oedipus at Colonus* in 1978]? I don't remember.

Tanya: There was a lot of argument about what we were going to use and one or two people wanted to use something that had been invented—the name of which I'm happy to say I have forgotten, but it was synthetic. And when whoever was helping me with the masks plunged her hands into it, they practically dropped off. It was poisonous, toxic—

it was horrible. And she said, "I don't like this stuff, do you?" and I said "I hate it. I would never suggest anyone should work with it. Why not just use papier-mâché, which is newspaper torn up? It's cheap enough, and dipped into paste or water, and several layers of that, and follow it with a layer of muslin and finish it off with a sort of smooth surface'. Wow, was that ever a good idea.

And I was only quoting what we'd done before, and what you've done before quite often works. I remember saying to you when I first arrived [in Adelaide], it was Christmastime...

Colin: Yes, it was just after Christmas [1977].

Tanya: I said something like: "You know what you asked for—it's going to take at least six months to prepare".

And you answered swiftly: "Well, we've got six weeks, so you'd better get on with it!' [laughter]

So, there wasn't much time for arguing with prop makers or mask makers—it was like "Try and let's see if it works. If it does, go into production".

Poster for Oedipus the King *and* Oedipus at Colonus, *Adelaide State Theatre Company, 1978*

And everybody worked overtime. One chap who was into hats found himself making shoes. And he thought "Well, I can do both". Well, of course, once he got into the shoe business, he became the cobbler of all time. Those terrible boots! Those cothurni and everything. But I think we were ready the first time. I know that Derek…

Colin: Derek was the production manager. Are you thinking of Dennis Olsen [who played Oedipus]?

Tanya: Who fell and sprained his ankle or something, but took no notice of that, "I'll be all right", and got on with it. But it seemed so awful because as you know Oedipus had bad feet! He didn't have to overdo it! [laughter]

But you had a wonderful cast. They were so polished, and they didn't complain. If they did it was behind locked doors, I never heard it.

Colin: I think I would have heard of it in due course. One other question out of interest, about 'Guinness's Yard'. Do you want to tell the story yourself? It was at the end of the first season [in Stratford in 1953].

Tanya: Oh, well. The thing was—I don't think I stayed to the end of the six weeks, or whatever it was. But Alec Guinness was asked point-blank if he had any criticisms or ideas he'd like to share for the future because he knew he wasn't coming back. And he said, "Yes I do. I do have a definite note I could give to the architects or to you Tanya or whoever's listening. When I'm on the flat stage, or quite a big portion of it, I always wanted to take one more step on that level before I went down, but it wasn't to be".

And so, we said, "Well, it's all going to be put away for the winter and rebuilt for next season."

"Next season – will there be one?"

"So, we'll add an extra length and call it 'The Guinness Step', I think, I've forgotten, 'The Guinness Yard' you call it. Whichever it was, it was incorporated. And, of course, it made a slight difference to the conformation, but it worked.

Colin: Is there anything else you remember—there's a Dame Sybil [Thorndike] story about masks and Lewis Casson at Minneapolis.[11]

Tanya: Oh, that's a big jump. But you saw *The House of Atreus* [at the Guthrie Theater in 1967], so you knew exactly what I mean when everybody was masked up to the eyebrows. Whether they had claustrophobia or not... One of them did, we

---

[11] Sybil Thorndike (1882-1976) and Lewis Casson (1875-1969) were the leading theatre couple of their generation, acting in and directing numerous productions during their long careers.

didn't know that but one of them was shrieking and we thought it was good acting. Robin Gammell was wonderfully helpful with his appearance.[12] He joined in, as it were...

Colin: He was Cassandra.

Tanya: ...being absolutely in tune with the look of the character. He put all the colours of the rainbow in this vegetable dye and all of them together they turned out to make it black, which was terrible because he didn't know it would. And he then rinsed his mouth out with that and appeared with a great hollow black inside to his mouth and teeth which was wonderful.

The management gave me the most awful telling-off and said Equity will kill you for having told an actor he had to do that. And I said I talked to the actor, and it was his idea and I went along with it because it's wonderful. And I wish everyone would do it, but they won't and they're not going to answer to me. But when Gammell opens his mouth [as Cassandra] and shouts... he made that his own. I admired him immensely for that. But all the actors brought something to their appearance.

---

[12] Robin Gammell is a Canadian film, television and stage actor who has performed on thrust stages around the world.

Colin: I remember you said something about Sir Lewis Casson?

Tanya: Yes, Lewis said to me: "I'd like to give you a note," at the dress rehearsal.

And I said: 'Of course what is it?"

And he said: "I think that actor (pointing to Gammell) is wonderful, but I can't really see his face very well because the colour of the mask makes him somewhat invisible".

He was quite an old man, his eyesight wasn't all that great, but it was a good comment. He said: "Would you think of repainting that?"

So, I went to Carolyn [Parker] who had done all the masks and told her this and she said: "Well, I've always thought it should have been darker" and she quickly, quickly changed the tone.

And it was Lewis Casson's note. Of course, I got Tony Guthrie to agree. "Sir Lewis would like to make a little alteration."

"Go right ahead, whatever he said."

I was so proud to be given a note by Sir Lewis himself.

Colin: And was it darker or lighter?

Tanya: Don't ask—it's a hundred years ago!

Colin: I only ask because Elaine [Garrard] is doing masks and she tends to put on an almost white base and then builds up.

Tanya: I can't honestly swear to it. Carolyn is dead and gone, so is Lewis.

Colin: You mentioned about Desmond Heeley—is there anything he contributed to this, apart from adulation and a total belief in it? I know that he loved the ceiling at the Crucible. Did he contribute at all to the design?[13]

Tanya: He did, in his own way. Until very recently he's contributed with his knowhow. He always knows what things should look like. It doesn't always work out that way, but he's got very high ideals and so he's very practical: he knows what can and can't be done. I used to lean heavily on him. But his story is that he leant on me. Well, between us we did a great leaning act! I was a great deal older than

---

[13] Editor's note: British set designer, Desmond Heeley, made two key contributions to the Crucible's design. First, he recommended that the vomitories (tunnels) meet the corners of the thrust stage at 45-degree angles; this gave the thrust stage two axes crossing at right angles in the 'Sacred Circle' and dictated the octagonal shape of the auditorium. Second, he designed a magical sorcerer, 'The Enchanter', which hung above the main foyer staircase during the opening years of the Crucible.

him—I had been at it a lot longer. But he was full of, shall I say, enthusiasm but it didn't just end there.

It was, "If you want it changed, speak up and I'll back you up and we'll change it, or we'll talk ourselves into it". And he was very cooperative.

Colin: Anything to say of Dougie Campbell?

Tanya: Well, only that he was a forceful energy. Anything that was lackadaisical was out. You had to be absolutely on top form and ready to see his point of view, which usually was pretty good, and I loved working with him and for him. But every now and then I'd really test him, almost to screaming: "No, no, you can do that!"

And Douglas, when he was Pallas Athena in this terrible get-up that Guthrie and I made between us, and when he got into it—he was strapped in practically—he said Tony Guthrie had been trying to do this to him for years! And then he turned to—he had four, not train bearers, but they carried him, they lifted the whole edifice onto the stage with a lot of dry ice and that. And he said: "Don't leave me! Don't leave me!" And he really panicked inside this thing. It wasn't claustrophobia, he just thought there's going to be a fire, everyone will leave the building and he'll still be there! But he wasn't. He was never left.

Colin: Is there anything you'd like to add about the Crucible? I'm writing a book about it.[14]

Tanya: Well, I got into a very high state of excitement that there was going to be a theatre. You and David Brayshaw[15] had been to America and Canada, and between you decided that the kind of stage you wanted was the open stage and not another proscenium stage—which may or may not have overexcited Bernard Miles. He dashed into print to say terrible things which was enough to make you want it all the more. You were sold on the idea—you'd seen it work. So, I enjoyed being in Sheffield and being part of all that. But once the stage was ready to be acted on you and David said: "Now we have built the theatre, you've got to prove that you can work in it, so will you stay?"

And I said: "Ooohhh! Why not? I'd love to!"

And you said: "Do a couple of shows and then we'll talk about it again".

---

[14] This became *Stirring Up Sheffield: An insider's account of the battle to build the Crucible Theatre*, Wordville, November 2021.

[15] David Brayshaw was Chairman of the Executive Committee of the Sheffield Playhouse Board and later became the first Administrator of the Crucible Theatre (1971-75).

        Later it was like: "I don't think we can afford to pay you anymore, so you'd better leave now!"

Colin: I remember that they were so short of money and decided to get rid of the Design Consultant and I handed in my resignation. And then I got the whole company together and said, "I'm not going next week, I'm going in 18 months' time. I must move on, but I don't want there to be any false rumours as happens in the theatre. And you were there.

        I asked what you thought and you said, "It was fine, but it was like the captain saying I'm leaving the ship at such and such a time."

Tanya Moiseiwitsch's central design for The Persians
at the Crucible Theatre (Sheffield), October 1972

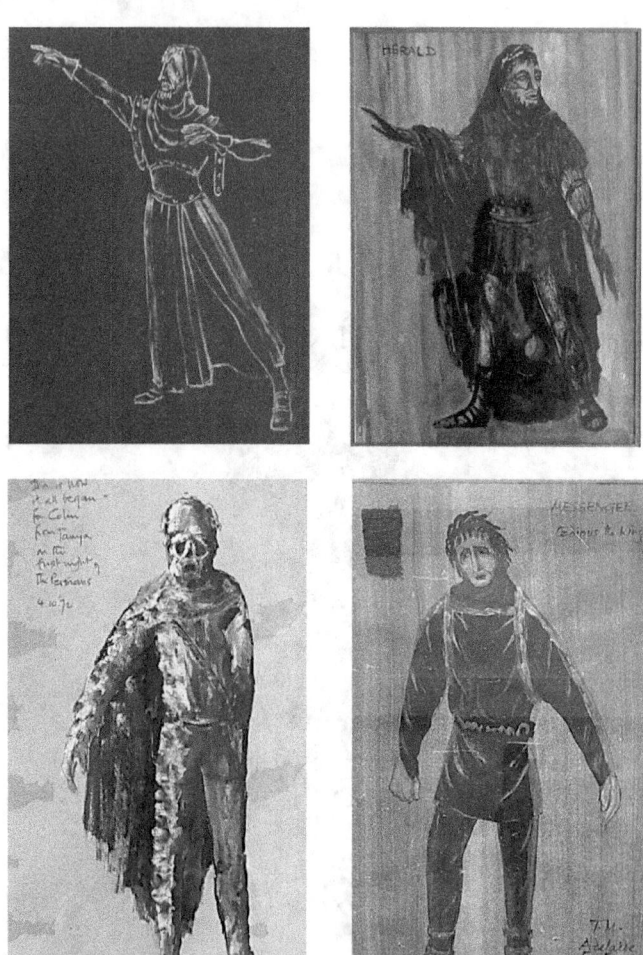

Tanya's designs for the Messenger over the years (clockwise from top left): King Oedipus *(1954),* The House of Atreus *(1967),* Oedipus The King *(1978) and* The Persians *(1972).*

www.ingramcontent.com/pod-product-compliance
Lightning Source LLC
Chambersburg PA
CBHW050256120526
44590CB00016B/2373